BOYS
A Schoolmaster's Journal

Boys
A Schoolmaster's Journal

Ronald Bazarini

Walker and Company
New York

For Corinna Manetto

First published in the United States of America in 1988 by the Walker Publishing
Company, Inc.
Published simultaneously in Canada by Thomas Allen & Son
Canada, Limited, Markham, Ontario.

Library of Congress Cataloging-in-Publication Data

Bazarini, Ronald
    Boys : a schoolmaster's journal / Ronald Bazarini.
        p.   cm.
    ISBN 0-8027-1053-0
    1. St. Bernard's School (Manhattan, New York, N.Y.) 2. Bazarini, Ronald. 3.
Elementary school teachers—New York (N.Y.)—Biography. 4. Preparatory school
students—New York (N.Y.) I. Title.
LD7501.N526B39   1988   88-10807
372.11'0092'4—dc19   CIP

Permissions:

p. 18: John Peal Bishop, quoted from "The Hunchback" in THE COLLECTED
    POEMS OF JOHN PEAL BISHOP, edited by Allen Tate. Copyright 1948
    Charles Scribner's Sons; copyright renewed © 1976 Charles Scribner's
    Sons. Reprinted with the permission of Charles Scribner's Sons, an imprint
    of Macmillan Publishing Company.
p. 18: "Willy Wet Leg" by D. H. Lawrence. From THE COMPLETE POEMS OF D.
    H. LAWRENCE, edited by Vivian de Sola Pinto and F. Warren Roberts.
    Copyright © 1964, 1971 by Angelo Ravagli and C. M. Weekley, executors
    of the estate of Frieda Lawrence Ravagli. All right reserved. Reprinted by
    permission of Viking Penguin Inc. and Laurence Pollinger Ltd.
    Excerpt from "Help," "Opera Notes," "A Sharing," "A Journal Entry" by
    Ronald Bazarini. Copyrights 1984, 1980, 1970, 1978 by Ronald Bazarini.
    Reprinted by perimssion of THE INDEPENDENT SCHOOL.

Text design by Laurie McBarnette
Printed in the United States of America

10 9 8 7 6 5 4 3 2 1

I remember the gleams and glooms that dart
Across the school-boy's brain;
The song and the silence in the heart....

—Henry Wadsworth Longfellow, "My Lost Youth"

Contents

Preface

Occasionally, I manage to spend a year at home writing, but for eighteen years I've taught the fourth grade at St. Bernard's School, a grammar school for boys.

This book is about the rascality, the wonder and the laughter of childhood I found there.

It is also a sharing.

To mothers, fathers, and teachers I offer the joy and the insights my nine-year-old charges have given me.

To do this I must speak of the successes and the difficulties of children, but, of course, I have no intention of writing about any child's personal life. Consequently, all of the children and all of the parents in this book are not real people; they have been created by me and placed into scenes, into situations that disclose the thoughts and feelings of the child. The exception is the scene called "Style." It happened exactly as depicted and the boys carry their real names. Also, the pieces titled "Alimony" and "The Vestal Virgin" were written by the fourth-graders credited.

As for the faculty and my family, it has been my privilege to use, with their permission, their real names. I wanted their company.

Ronald Bazarini

Childhood: Jail

The attractive mother of a robust, worthwhile hellion is seated before me in my classroom at St. Bernard's. I am her son's fourth-grade teacher. We are having a parent conference.

"We must remember," I say, "your child didn't choose to be your child, and he didn't choose to be my student."

She asks, "What are you talking about?"

It's true, I think, I have been abrupt. More slowly I continue, "He didn't choose us but nonetheless he must put up with us."

"You mean he doesn't like me?" Her blue eyes seem rounder than most people's.

"I mean he'd prefer that his mother lived on a raft floating down the Mississippi. He'd prefer to hunt alligators than attend the fourth grade. Instead he's stuck with a mother who sells bonds and a teacher who reads Henry James."

"To the boys?"

"What?"

"You read Henry James to the boys?"

"No, to myself. A little at a time." I pause. "The point is, he's stuck with us whether we make him happy or sad, confident or despondent, open or closed. He can't tip his hat like an adult and say, 'I'm sorry, Mom. Sorry, sir. This isn't working. I'm leaving!'"

We take a moment.

She adjusts the sling of her shoe.

"You make childhood sound like jail."

"Exactly," I answer. "We are his jailers and we must make

the jailing as humane as possible. Not liberty to the point of license, but as much consideration as we can muster. Always ready to give him freedom when we safely can."

She blinks and asks, "Do you have children of your own, Mr. Bazarini?"

"I do," I say.

"You don't sound like it."

"I know. I think I'm trying to redefine fatherhood, redefine teacherhood." I look for the words. "Because I don't think we do right by our children. Especially these days. There's so much stress in our daily lives, so much to contend with, it makes us go astray. The children have to cope not only with their own anxieties but also with our disabilities."

I stop and then repeat, "We must do right by the child. 'The child is sacred.' "

She says, "He's also a huge pain."

"Your child."

"Mine."

"I've noticed."

 ## Prompting

This dream keeps occurring.

I've been having it ever since I began teaching my fourth-graders Roman history.

It takes place in Florence. I'm in a dark corner of a crumbling secondhand store that specializes in small sculptures. No one is near me, no one sees me. The floor stone feels loose beneath my foot and suddenly it gives way! One end of it sinks six inches beneath level. I, alone, know what has happened. As I go down on one knee instinctively to set it properly, I see within the underspace a shallow, narrow box containing a sheaf of papers. Carefully, I get my hand under

2

it and pull it out. The papers are a journal written in the time of ancient Rome. It's a teacher's journal, the story of his daily endeavors, his thoughts about children, his attitudes toward their parents—his experiences, hopes and perceptions.

I'm thrilled to have uncovered it.

I take it to the store owner, a middle-aged, red-headed, fair-skinned woman peeling peaches. It is a slow, stately walk. She receives me with deep-set piercing eyes.

"I found this beneath the floor," I say. "It was written in ancient times. It's the record of a teacher."

"Good," she says simply. "Maybe he knows how to make the children behave."

"Or how we should behave towards the children. How much?"

She hesitates. I feel foolish. It's much too precious. She'll never sell it.

"The box included?" she says.

"Yes."

"Fourteen hundred lire. I'd sell it for less, but it could be important."

"I think it is."

"I'm glad for you."

Out on the street, I hold the book in my arm and stop to contain my delight. I look through the store window to wave goodbye to the owner. She doesn't see me. She is talking to her dog.

 ## Interview

Mrs. Ashton, a gray-haired English lady, is the first to greet me when I enter St. Bernard's.

"Do you mind, Mr. Bazarini? Mr. Fry will be another ten

minutes. He suggests you stroll about the school."

"Thank you, I will."

She disappears into a first-grade room.

It is bleak. The entire school is dreary—black and brown floor tiles, beige walls, cramped quarters, dust, and no sign of sunlight. I read it for what it is: British highmindedness. "We have better things to think about here." But my Adriatic blood, my Illyrian soul, yearns for splashing blue water and green and white ceramics. Just some. The English, I like them so, their tailoring, their furniture, their paintings and prose...but St. Bernard's is bleak.

When I return to the main hallway, I'm greeted by Turgenev, the divine Ivan. He is extremely tall, his hair is silver and full, he is soft-spoken, gentlemanly, and reeks of pen and paper. But it is not Ivan, it is the Englishman Humphrey Fry.

"Ronald, I'm so glad you could come."

We've never met before yet he speaks to me as if we've spent our last holiday playing croquet on the Isle of Skye.

"Over here, Ronald, we'll sit in the headmaster's office. I'm sure he won't mind. He's on sabbatical, you know. I'm doing the interviewing this spring. Sit down, please."

It takes him no more than a minute to make me want to teach at St. Bernard's or die. I feel at home with him. The delight of it makes me smile. I like being a street kid from the French Quarter of New Orleans. I also like having made it to Yale and Stanford. The span of it is appealing and never more appealing than now seated opposite this huge, cultured, humorous man of letters.

As a young actor, I remember my fellow actors yearning to study the Method with Strasberg and speak like Marlon Brando. But what I wished for was an invitation to spend the summer in Charles de Gaulle's chateau.

4

Not for the snobbishness of it.

For the experience.

For the stretch of it.

I knew about torn T-shirts and inner feelings, strong feelings; I knew about Tennessee Williams's French Quarter—I was born in it; I knew about the emotionalism of uneducated people and I knew of their grace and simplicity and blessedness. They were my family and I cherished them.

But I wanted more.

I wanted to know about the emotional life of those to the manner born; I wanted to know about subtlety, too, and propriety and polished expression.

Not to give up one for the other.

I wanted both.

The school would be a finishing school for me. The term doesn't embarrass me. I need some finishing.

Yet, I'm worried.

I know these Englishmen and Englishwomen who come to the colonies to try their hand. I know New Yorkers fall at their feet because of their accent. I couldn't do that. Far too proud. I acknowledge their superior polish but I'm fully aware of the worth of American straight talk and natural ways.

Humphrey's been going through my resumé.

It's scant—but I have mentioned my Rockefeller Grant to Yale and my Honors Scholarship to Stanford's graduate school. I don't mean to brag but use the little I've got.

"Ronald," he asks, "why do you want to be a teacher?"

"For the vacation," I answer.

"The time off?"

"Yes. To write."

"You're a writer."

"In the oven."

"Splendid."

He's delighted but not in any great spontaneous way. More like a tourist in Martinique who discovers by chance that the price of his room includes three meals a day. One shouldn't act as if one didn't expect it.

"I think you'll like it here."

"I know I will."

He rises to his full six feet, six inches height. He is the most impeccably well-dressed man I've ever seen.

"I hope you don't ask for much salary?"

"No. Enough to live on."

"Good."

We don't talk of anything else.

The interview is over.

He wishes me a productive summer and looks forward to seeing me in September.

I'm hired.

Influence

She's good-looking in the best of ways—outside there is minimum allure but inside there's character. The kind of face that will look better at sixty than it did at twenty.

She has seated herself in a child's chair next to my big green teacher's chair.

"How are you?" she asks.

"I do look older, don't I?"

She's quick to smile. "Do you mean Harry?"

"Your son's wearing me out."

She laughs easily. "Do you mind if I smoke?"

"Here's a cup for an ashtray. Harry's in a tailspin."

"That last report was terrible."

"And what's he like at home?"

"He's very tough on me. I don't seem to do anything right."

I open the window a bit.

I ask, "Does Ernest come over much to play?"

She's glad I brought up the subject.

"You knew? I wanted to talk to you about that. Mr. Bazarini, I hope I'm not talking out of turn, but I've never known a child like Ernest before. And my son adores him."

"I know."

"We took Ernest with us to Bermuda during spring break and the child didn't bathe for a week. He didn't swim and he didn't bathe for a week. He was pale gray."

"He's a free spirit."

"But, Mr. Bazarini, Harry did the same. We had to eat in outdoor restaurants. I finally grabbed my child and threw him into the sea."

"Ernest is charismatic."

"My husband got very upset."

"At Ernest?"

"At me."

I nod sympathetically. "Whatever you do, don't get mad at Harry."

"I know that."

"It's the call of the wild. Harry is captivated by Ernest's courage."

"I understand that."

"I'm sure you can remember being attracted by a girlfriend who was reckless."

"I can," she says, "but I didn't stop bathing."

She laughs wide-eyed and shakes her head in wonderment.

I ask, "Did you ask Ernest to bathe?"

"I did. I asked him to bathe, to stop eating with his hands, to stop sleeping on the floor."

"What did he say?"

"He said I wasn't his mother. I said 'Do you behave when she asks you to?' He said, 'No.' I said, 'Why not?' He said it was a free world."

"Intractable. I call him Ernest the Intractable."

"Is he like that in class?"

"No. He loves to learn. Does quite well. It's between classes you have to watch him. Between the ending of one class and the beginning of the next, Ernest enters the Twilight Zone. The world becomes primal. There are no laws to follow. Power rules."

"But, I thought you meant—don't you mean my son's—ah—slump I think you said, is Ernest's fault?"

"Directly connected to Ernest."

"But you say Ernest does fine in class?"

"He does. For some reason he turns off his crazies when he's in class. But your son is still impressed with Ernest's fresh answer to the gym teacher during the game, or with the way Ernest tripped the sixth-grader on the back steps. Your son doesn't know how to turn it off. The wild pressure of it. He still wants to laugh and slide about. It takes him fifteen minutes to recover. Then he spends the next fifteen minutes trying to imagine what Ernest will do at lunch."

"Lunch? Don't mention lunch! The last time he was over for lunch he made a mashed-potato sandwich. What do you suggest?"

"I'd hate to deprive Harry of Ernest. Fun never comes so pure ever again. What about your girlfriend? How did you handle that?"

"The last time I was with her she started shoplifting men's ties in Bendel's."

"You went your own way."

"Yes. Should I forbid Harry to see him?"

"Don't do that. You'll create a dark hero. Don't even

mention Ernest. Just find reasons to keep him at a distance. People without restraint fascinate us."

 ## Safety

Anthony's mother and father have come to confer. Today is their eleventh wedding anniversary.

She begins. "Anthony's father and I—well—the whole reason we thought to send him to St. Bernard's was to make him a gentleman."
He says, "And he's roaming all over town. Don't kids have to go home after school?"
"Yes," I say. I like the daddy. He has a refreshing way of not thinking before he speaks.
"Well, Anthony doesn't."
"Anthony's free!" I say it meaning Anthony's glorious.
He understands. He smiles and answers, "That's it!"
"Were you?" I ask.
"Me?" He looks at his wife. "I went to school in New Jersey."
"Public school?"
"Yes."
"Did you roam all over town?"
"Yes," he answers.
"So your kid's like you."

Mother doesn't like the turn of the conversation.
"But," she says, "it isn't safe."
"No," I reply, "it isn't. And I mean to talk to Anthony and try to get him to go straight home after school. There's something admirable about him."
Dad says, "He's a take-charge kid."

"Yes," I answer. "He believes in himself. He has no fear."

Father likes hearing this. He knows fearlessness and will-fulness can be dangerous to a child but he also knows they can build self-reliance.

He looks at me thoughtfully and says, "But I can't take it. I worry too much about him. Do fourth-graders get picked up after school?"

"One or two."

"I'll send my sister," he says.

"I have to work till six," she explains.

"He'll hate it," I say.

"I know that," the father says. "I don't want to make him mad, either. He's a good kid."

"Let's give it a try," I say. "Tell your sister to come. Tell her to treat him, the movies, pizza—spoil him till he gets used to the idea."

She starts, "Isn't that..."

"Bribing him?" I say.

"Yes."

"Think of it as a reward. Or think of it as a trick. Sometimes we've got to trick each other."

"Anthony?" he says. "Anthony knows every trick in the book."

When they're gone, I think of myself as a parent, I think of the fierce protectiveness I feel for my sons.

Mothers and fathers are all alike that way.

I think of a friend who teaches at one of our most prestigious universities. He is an authority on a great novelist, a novelist whose gift as a writer seems to have grown out of his tortured life. The novelist is trenchant because he suffered the torment of seeing too clearly, of understanding too much. My friend devotes his life to the memory of this novelist. I remember telling him, "But you sacrifice your own creative writing to write about him."

"He's worth it," he answered. "He's glorious. He faced the

10

dread of life to bring back perceptions!"

I asked, "Would you like one of your children to be that gifted?"

"At that price?"

"Yes."

"No. No, please. I want my children happy."

We're all alike, parents.

We want our children forever safe, eternally happy, clean, and blissfully content.

To hell with adventure.

To hell with greatness.

 Style

To go home in the afternoon, I ride the 96th Street crosstown bus through Central Park and then catch the IND subway downtown.

Once I board the subway, the next stop is 86th Street. This morning I hear a radio announcer say there has been a fellow showing up at that station with a hatchet and an angry disposition.

That's why I take a different way home today.

I catch the Fifth Avenue downtown bus.

As I'm getting my transfer from the driver, I hear from the back of the bus, "Hey, Baz!"

It's one of my fourth-graders, a kid named Nick Judson. Sitting next to him is Trip, another member of our class.

"Hey," I say and make my way back to sit with them. "I thought you walked home, Trip."

"I'm going to Nick's house."

"Great."

11

Trip is conservative and industrious. Nick is free-wheel-ing. He dresses as he pleases—checkered hightop sneakers, and he cuts his hair short and slicks it back. He's a bright kid who has no interest in school. He's in trouble with all of his teachers but he somehow doesn't make anyone mad. For one thing he never gets ruffled. At least, he never shows it. He has a special look of confidence that has nothing in-subordinate about it. He's smooth. He's a successful, prag-matic businessman waiting to come of age.

After we chat for a few minutes, he says, "Baz, would you like to stop off and have a drink with us?" He says it as simp-ly and as friendly to me as a thirty-year-old stockbroker would say it to a colleague.

He captivates me. This independent, low-keyed, nine-year-old boy invites me for an afternoon drink and I am thoroughly pleased.

"Sure. Love to." I have no idea what he has in mind but I'll follow Nick to the end of the earth.

He looks out of the bus window as we approach the Metropolitan Museum. "Will the Stanhope do?"

The Stanhope is a chic, understated, "in" New York hotel on Fifth opposite the museum.

"Perfect," I say. I visualize myself and two nine-year-old boys entering the bar and I can't wait for it to happen. Nick is cool. Trip and I are acting cool.

Trip and I follow him into the hotel. He knows his way around. He turns right. We turn right. He enters the hotel lounge and says to me, "I like this corner table."

"All right by me," I say and sit across from him. Trip sits between us, as pleased as punch. As the waitress ap-proaches, Nick says, "Trip and I are having Cokes but you can have something stronger if you like."

"Coke is fine, Nick."

"Hello, Nick," says the waitress. She's all smiles.

Nick says, "Three Cokes, please."
"Be right back," she says and leaves.

Obviously Nick is known here. Obviously he's got a tab. I settle back and we talk about the Mets and the Yankees. Trip loves the Yankees, I love the Mets, Nick is too good a businessman to tip his hand. He has something discerning to say about each team and orders another round.

We have a great discussion on Steinbrenner. Trip and I hate him. Nick says Steinbrenner has a business to run.
I get high on the caffeine.
I talk too much.
I look at my watch. "Geez, I'd better get home! Thanks, Nick, Trip."
Nick says, "See you in class, Baz."

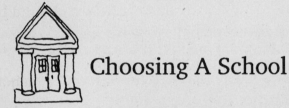

Choosing A School

My friend Robert transfers whipped cream from the top of his lemon mousse to the top of his coffee. We're seated at a table overlooking Madison Avenue.

"I thought you'd be some help," he says.
"Robert, I don't know about girls' schools."

Robert and I met in college. Next year his daughter will be ready to enter kindergarten. He and his wife have been visiting several grammar schools.

I ask, "Did you poke into any classes?"
"Yes," he answers. "What does that tell you? A perfectly quiet, beautiful-to-look-at class may be a stifled class."

13

"Could be."

He offers me some of his lemon-tainted whipped cream for my coffee. "Try it."

"No, thanks. What about laughter?"

"You mean if you hear laughter from a class that's a good sign?"

"Yes."

"Suppose the teacher's being sarcastic?"

"Could be."

"Come on, Ronny-bob, the teacher could be making fun of a kid. Let's be serious. There's no way to tell a good school."

"Be careful."

"Be careful! That's what I'm trying to be! Do you realize my wife and I have spent the last year and a half casing grammar schools? All of our new tennis partners are people we met visiting grammar schools!"

"It's important," I say.

His face reddens. "Ronald, I know it's important. Now, will you try to think of something to say I don't already know?"

"Victoria will spend more time at her grammar school than she'll spend at any other school!"

He's talking to himself. "A huge part of my little Vickie's life."

"And Goethe says we base our philosophy on our life's experiences!"

He hasn't heard.

Either that or he can't believe I alluded to Goethe.

"What?"

"I was agreeing with you, Robert."

"With what?"

"Grammar school is where a child attains consciousness."

"Oh, God, Ronald, don't make it any more serious than it is."

"It's there a child becomes aware decisions can be his own."

"See," he says. "That's what I missed going to the dump I went to. I can't make a Goddamn decision!"

"I'm trying to help."

"What have you told me?"

"Just be sure the teachers are good and are allowed to teach the way each teaches best. That's what I'd look for."

"Who tells you if the teachers are good?"

"The headmaster."

"And if he lies?"

"Then I wouldn't trust him."

He doesn't laugh.

"You're not a serious person, Ronald."

"Check the hallways," I say, inspired. "Kids in the hallways are themselves. If they're full of bounce and schemes, it's probably a happy school."

"Did Barbara Walters go to a happy school?"

"Robert! Vickie is five years old!"

"That's when you start, Ronald. If you want to be America's spokeswoman you start at five."

 Poets

I met a poet in San Francisco.

His name was Brian.

I was a destitute actor at the time and I felt right at home in Brian's apartment, which was always filled with stricken artists.

He was a tough customer, Brian, and so were the measure of poets that banded round him. They were a competitive bunch filled with what Bernard Shaw refers to as the Life Force.

On Thursday nights they gathered in one or the others's heatless living rooms to read aloud their latest poems. They were fraught evenings. They had a tumble and a push about them. A tall poet would stand and shout his poem to life as if he wanted all of California to hear; a spectacled poet would mutter his stanzas, but mutter them fiercely; a Mexican fellow with a Spanish *S* would speak his sweetly, sweetly but somehow equally fierce.

They would jeer more than praise, talk more than listen.

Get four or five life forces bounding about the same room and you have a competition.

For having known them, I read poetry differently. I sense in Emily Dickinson the determination of Hannibal.

Grace held in strong hands.

Opinion, too, strong opinion enhanced with insight.

It's a rough existence, that of a poet: the tearing away of all that clouds vision and then the wrestling with what one does see.

All of it makes me wonder if Clifford is a poet?

For a fourth-grader, Clifford is a tough customer; he's wiry, sallow-cheeked, brown-eyed, and oriented toward the take-down. He has the pent-up aura of a failed Zen priest assigned to tending the monastery's back garden.

As for his life force, I'd pit his against any two of those San Francisco poets.

He may be a poet.

That may be why he is especially restless during the time the class spends on a scheme I've developed over the years called the Poetry Notebook, a mighty enterprise for nine-year-olds, a grand attempt to submerge ourselves in a year's long effort to come nose-to-nose with thought balanced in meter, with thought forcefully condensed.

Clifford has trouble with it.

If he is a poet he may have too much poetry already within his nine-year-old soul. If that is so, he damn well may resent the intrusion of another's insights, no matter how gracefully held.

I wonder.

For example, this kid Chris—a kid who's been given a headstart on his homework because he works slowly—throws down his pencil triumphantly and then begins to brag about finishing first.

I say, "Hold on, buddy!"

The moment I do, Clifford raises his head and looks at me in challenge. He knows that I'm about to take issue with Chris for bragging. Clifford senses that I've sensed a moral moment.

I have.

I say to Chris, "Chris, even though you crossed the line first, you didn't really win the race."

Chris doesn't know what I'm talking about but Clifford does. Clifford says, "Why not? Why didn't he win?"

"Because, Clifford," I say, robed in white, "he had a headstart!"

"All right, but he actually did win."

"How's that?"

"Because, sir," he explained, "he crossed the line first and that's what counts!"

"Clifford," I ask, "if you were on the United States Olympic basketball team and you had the chance the night before the game to poison the food of the entire opposing team—"

"The Russians?"

"Whoever."

"I'd do it!"

I pause and then continue. "I know. My question is: the next day when they show up deathly ill and you beat them by thirty points, would you *enjoy* the victory?"

"Sure."

"How could you, Clifford?"
"Why not?"
"You poisoned them!"
"Sir, it's the Olympics! The point is to win."

He smiles when he says it.
He looks around the class for approval.
"He's right, sir," says one kid.
"He is, sir," says another.
That's about right. Every year about three kids out of twenty agree with that attitude.
"The point is to win."
He says it coldly, as a statement of fact, a steady cool spreading out before me of reality. Clifford's force, his coolness, his look into what is—much like a poet.

The Poetry Notebook takes the full school year to complete. First, a poem is selected. Sometimes for the laughter of it:

> I can't stand Willy Wet-leg
> can't stand him at any price.
> He's resigned, and when you hit him
> he lets you hit him twice.

That's by D.H. Lawrence.
Clifford likes that one.
Sometimes I choose one for the grit of it.
Here's a part of John Peale Bishop's poem, "The Hunchback":

> And I saw his face as he passed me by
> And the hateful look of his dead-fish eye...

> I watched him till his work was done;
> And suddenly God went out of the sun...

Sometimes for the rich ache of it,
Emily Dickinson:

The murmur of a bee
A witchcraft yieldeth me.
If any ask me why,
'Twere easier to die
Than tell.

Slowly, phrase by phrase, I dictate Miss Dickinson's poem. It comes to them through space, through sound they must catch. Clifford listens along with the rest.

"It's never easy to die," he says. "Why would she rather die than tell? Tell what?"

Courageously he brings his young boy's bravery to contest ideas with Emily Dickinson. She would have loved it. I can see the two of them in my poet friend's San Francisco living room, fighting for time to speak.

But during recess after lunch, he pushes a boy on an opposing touch-football team to the ground. He does it after the play is over. The boy had intercepted a pass meant for him, and in his frustration he pushes him to the ground.

Clifford is not a mean child. He is not the type to hatch an evil design. He just wants to win. He is possessed with the thought of winning. It makes him glow. The boys in the class follow him wherever he leads; they follow with abandon. He is the union boss whose thrust is never slowed by moral musings. He's a kid who loves to laugh. And argue.

When he throws the kid unfairly to the deck, I yell at him, "You can't do that!" I'm incensed.

He doesn't hear me. He's overcome with the defeat of the play. There's no chance he can understand my righteousness. I say, "Do you see what you did?" He blinks and wanders a bit, looks away and sits down against the fence.

"You're out of the game for five plays!"

He hears that.

"Why?"

"You haven't understood a word!"

He hasn't.

And minutes later, back in the game, still smarting, he starts an argument with the kid who intercepted the pass.

"No!" I yell. "No more recess for a week!"

I am not at my best. In the weeks gone by I have tried twenty times over to speak calmly to him of ethics but now he knows I am not at my best. My white robe is off. I'm ankle deep in the mud of reality. And it impresses him. He stands up to me like a fury but he's impressed. His tall, slight frame is rigid with argument. He won't consider morality. He insists winning is all. We both fume, and he is impressed. He hears me.

The heady stuff of poetry?
Listening.
Spelling.
Defining.
Musing.
Where has it all gone?

The next day his father calls.

"What's happening?" He's calling from work. "He didn't want to go to school today."

"We're fighting," I say.

"Fighting?"

"Yes. Over a principle! And it's no fun," I add.

"He's a kid!"

"A tough kid!"

He keeps talking.

I keep talking.

He gets excited.

I get excited.

We sound like the poets in San Francisco.

The following day, Clifford and I are cool. He draws a picture of murmuring bees and pastes it in his Poetry Notebook.

"Why do I have to memorize it?"

"Don't."

"Why does anyone?"

"To introduce careful cadence and the piercing economy of words into your brain." I say this to a nine-year-old. I must be crazy. "And we'll recite it to reach for poise!"

Clifford's disgusted.
We don't speak for two days.
I decide he's definitely not a poet.

Am I on an ego trip?
No.
I know I'm not for the sad reason that I've been there before. I've taken those trips both as a teacher and a father. I have experienced the terrible feeling of being personally insulted if a child didn't learn after *I* had taught him.
No.

With Clifford, I endeavor to bring him into awareness of right and wrong and not of my particular right and wrong. I think he should try to look upon actions within a judgment that attempts to consider how much self-appetite must be tempered with consideration for those who surround us.

It's clear that Clifford has yet to enter into this awareness. I don't know why. I do know he has decided he must depend on himself. He's manly. But all of it has made him too willful, too ready to fight.

Poets are willful, I'm sure of it. People provoked to spell it out their way, as they see it, must have strong wills. And they must be fighters, too.

But am I getting in over my head? Further down the road this courage, this strength will work to his advantage. But in the meantime, I see an unhappy child who can't understand why a courageous instinct is getting him into trouble. He indicates he'd like a change. I want to help him direct that force.

Am I tampering?
Am I getting too close to crossing over that line that separates helping from intrusion?
I'm not certain.
I do know that children judge us for how deep our feelings run. They look for a sense of conviction. A flawless explanation of "proper behavior" doesn't mean a thing to a child in trouble.

There's certainly no pleasure in it, this getting close. It would be the easiest thing in the world to let it pass. Easier on me. It's much like cleaning the dirt out of a child's scraped knee. Nobody likes it.
But it must be done.
You know that, and finally so does the child.

Clifford is tough.
Like poets.
And teaching is tough.

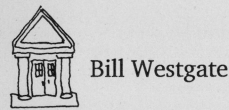 # Bill Westgate

When I arrived here over twenty years ago the school was headed by a Canadian named R.I.W. Westgate. He was as handsome as his string of initials was impressive. He was direct but cheerful, sharp on rare occasion, and always quick to appreciate.
He was a classical scholar, still is, tended bees, still does,

and he was also a perceptive headmaster, responsive to colleagues, trustees, parents, and children.

As a younger man, he walked and bussed through Greece with his bride Sheila and lectured on places and events from the yacht *Prince Olav*.

I see him coming into my room during the spring term of my first year.

"Hello, Baz."

"Good morning, Mr. Westgate."

"The boys treating you well?"

"Fine. They're off to the field."

"All seems to be in order."

"Yes, sir."

He is perfect casting.

Rugged good looks, piercing blue eyes, professorial dignity, and abounding vigor.

"Have you had a look at those ERBs, Baz?"

"Yes, sir."

"You know how to give them?"

"I think so."

"Good. We must give them every so often. Quite a lot we can learn from the scores."

"Standard testing."

"That's it."

He hesitates. Then he appears shy. He hasn't ever talked to me about teaching. He thinks to do so is, by and large, presumptuous.

Whatever it is, he's gearing up to say something he feels is important.

"They allow us, these ERBs, to focus on particular problems, you know. The parts. The thing is—we shouldn't make too much of the parts. It's the total child—the child all of a piece—that's the task."

"Each boy individually."

"Yes. We mustn't insist Peter Drisdale become a top scholar. Our purpose is to make him the best Peter Drisdale he can be."

I think what he says is profound but I don't know how to let him know it.

"Well," he says, "you fit in quite naturally, Baz. I hope you mean to stay on."

"Next year I may even figure out what I'm doing."

He smiles.

"Oh, good. Good."

We chat a minute longer and he leaves.

I sit alone.

Complete the child.

Charlotte, Emily, and Anne come to mind.

I picture the three Brontë girls huddled over their books. Not the books they're famous for. I picture them little girls writing out their little-girl books, the ones they wanted so much to look like real books.

The belief in themselves.

The circle of support.

Under Bill Westgate we felt ourselves a family. He took us aside and talked to us quietly and energetically. His words made us feel appreciated and made us eager to hone ourselves.

A feeling of family. A rare blessing.

That's the concept. Family. The school must embrace, encourage, believe in, and support the child the way a loving family does, a family, to be sure, with high standards. And as one family is different from another, each school should be allowed its differences.

 Horikiri Story

The boys have come in from the field early. All of them have changed back into their regular clothes. We have twelve minutes before we should leave for lunch.

Billy says, "Tell us a story, sir."

"Yeah," say three or four more.

"All right."

This is a ritual with us. Whenever we have a few extra minutes unaccounted for I tell them a story. They suggest storytelling as often as they can because it kills time and takes us away from our lessons, but they also make the request because children love to hear stories. With great generosity, I oblige if I possibly can. To please them pleases me, but there is another reason. By telling stories throughout the year, I become the storyteller, and the children subconsciously tune in to the storyteller more quickly than they do to any other adult. They learn to listen to me. That helps in every subject each day of the year.

Billy says, "An army story, sir."

I've told them some of my army tales already. The Occupation of Japan, that was my tour of duty. After I joined up at seventeen (to get the G.I. Bill and go to college with it afterwards), the army trained me in six weeks and quickly shipped me to Japan so that a war veteran could return home. My army stories are therefore not about enemies and killing.

"Once," I begin, "when I was working for Intelligence in Yokohama, I was given a four-day pass and a jeep for having completed a comprehensive report. A big report. Everyone was pleased. Here, Baz, enjoy yourself. My boss, Major

25

Putnam, even got a reservation for me at a Japanese country inn outside Atami."

Billy says, "This is true, right?"

"Yes. All of my stories are true."

That is very important to them, that all of the stories I tell them are true. It doesn't matter how simple the story is—I tell one about buying a pair of shoes with my brother on his wedding day—as long as it is true.

They all sit quietly.

They know I'm a prima donna when I tell a story. If they squirm around, I stop.

"I picked up my jeep and drove through the soft, subtle countryside to this faraway old-fashioned inn. It was in Horikiri. It was built on the side of a mountain in the middle of pine trees. It was not a decorated place; it was not brightly colored. The wood was natural. It was plain but it was also stylishly handsome. Picture a fancy, new-built swimming pool, and then picture the bend of a lazy river where the kids like to swim in the summer. It was more like that river place. Only, it was on the side of a huge mountain and the mountain sloped down, quickly down, to the Pacific Ocean. From the inn, through the trees here and there, you could see bits of the Pacific sparkling in the sun."

"How long did you live there?"

"Four days."

"Great."

"My room was beautiful. I'll never forget how calm and clean it was, but it didn't have a bed. I had to sleep on a big quilt right on the floor. Except, the floor was made of straw mats and since you weren't allowed to walk around in your shoes, it was perfectly clean."

"Where did you leave your shoes?"

"I forget. Either outside the door of the room or outside downstairs. I forget. In the morning, that first morning, I was awakened by a beautiful young Japanese girl. She was so pretty, so smooth of face, I felt embarrassed because I was just seventeen still, and my face wasn't real clear and,

I don't know, I didn't feel as—as fine as she."

"What did she want?"

"She came to wake me up and bring a pitcher of water and a bowl and towel and soap so I could freshen up."

"Then you'd feel neat, too," says Joey.

"It helped. So, now I'm up and dressed and I've had breakfast. What am I going to do? I go outside and stand under the sweet-smelling trees. I get the idea to walk down the mountainside to the edge of the Pacific. Quickly I change into my sneakers and I'm on my way."

John says, "It's time for lunch, sir."

Billy says, "You idiot!"

John says, "He told me I'm the clock watcher."

"That's right, John. I'll finish the story tomorrow."

"When?"

"When I can. Now, quietly, line up."

Two days later.

"Where was I?"

"Your sneakers."

"Oh, yes. And it was a good thing I changed to my sneakers because the slope was steep. Carefully, I made my way down, so carefully that I didn't notice the water's edge until I practically got there. There was no beach. The mountain dropped directly into the ocean, and what separated the two was not a beach but a pile of red rocks. These were the biggest rocks I'd ever seen, and they were a dark red. One rock would fill up this room. Maybe two of the smallest ones. And there were hundreds and hundreds of them to the right. To the left, the mountain was separated from the ocean by only one huge rock. Past that rock I couldn't see, because the mountain jutted out there and hid the rest of itself.

"I couldn't wait to see what was on the other side of the mountain. I began jumping from one rock to the next to get closer to that final rock. The sun was shining bright, the sky was pure green-blazing blue, and the smell of the ocean was salty, pungent—it was a glorious morning."

"What was on the other side?" Joey asks this.

"Take it easy. The trouble is, to get to the other side of the mountain, I have to jump on that last huge rock and it is sticking so far out into the ocean that each wave breaks against it and sprays it completely. What I have to do is time it. I have to jump after one wave breaks and then jump off onto the other side of the mountain before the next wave arrives. Only thing is, what's on the other side? What is there to jump down upon?"

"What?"

"Joey, I'm getting to that."

"But we're gonna run out of time."

Billy says, "If you shut up maybe he can finish!"

"I time it and I jump. Quick! What's on the other side? By golly, there is a beach. Not a wide beach but the instant I jump on the red rock I see on the other side a narrow beach, real sand, that separates the other side of the mountain from the sea. Quick, I jump down onto the beach! Silence. I'm all alone. The mountain blocks away the red rocks and the inn. It's just me on the narrow beach at the foot of this gigantic mountain. I'm standing there in the sun, a mass of earth to one side, a massive sea to the other, and the blazing sky overhead. It's splendid. It's time for art."

"Huh?"

"Come on, sir!"

"I'm sorry, it's time for art. I'll finish tomorrow."

"That's what you always say."

"I promise."

The next day.

"I'm on the beach?"

"Right."

"Okay. I start to walk along the sand, the narrow strip of sand, a yellow ribbon between land and sea. After a while,

I see a hole."

"A cave?"

"I think so. But the opening isn't big. But if I stoop down and crawl on my hands and knees I can fit in. That's what I do. I crawl into this small opening because I have never been in a cave. Guess what happened?"

"What?"

"What?"

"A snake, right?"

"No, but I realize as soon as I'm in a few feet my body acts like a stopper and my body shuts out all of the light from outside. The deeper I crawl in, the darker it gets. Frightening. It's frightening. Part wants to backpedal out of there, another part of me wants to go further. Further in I go. Pitch black. And then a glint! What? Yes, again, a glint! I panic. I rear up to turn around but I can't. I hit my head on the top of the tunnel I'm in. I can't turn round. What is it? A flicker. It's a flicker.

"I calm myself and continue. Closer. Closer. It's a flame. It's a small flame from a candle, and there, behind the flame, is a smiling face. 'Come in,' it says. 'Come join me for tea!' "

"You're kidding, right sir?"

"No. This happened. Behind the flame sat a middle-aged Japanese man. The cave widened and got higher where he was just before it ended. He wouldn't have been able to stand, not quite, but he could sit comfortably and he could stretch out when he wanted to sleep."

"You mean he lived there?"

"Yes. He and his wife. He told me his wife had gone to the village for the day."

"What did you do?"

"I joined him for tea."

"You weren't afraid?"

"No more. He was too pleasant. He was sitting there writing. There were a few American action-story books at his side. He was translating."

"Why did he live there?"

"The war had just ended. The atom bomb had destroyed his city. He was poor and had no job. He found this place to live in until they could manage better."

"He spoke English?"

"Very well. He also wrote it and read it. Except he couldn't understand American slang."

"Like, 'cool, baby!' " Billy says that.

"Exactly. He asked me what 'engine-room stuff' meant. He said this sailor that worked below deck tells this sailor that works topside, 'You don't have that engine-room stuff it takes!' I helped him translate for an hour or more and then I left."

"What happened to him?"

"I don't know."

"Did you write him a letter?"

"No."

"Did you go back the next day?"

"No. I should have. I didn't."

"Did you like him?"

"Yes."

"Yeah. He sounds neat."

 Possessives and Poise

It's English class.

"So," I say, "the noun ends in a plural *s*. How would you make it possessive?"

Ernest raises his hand.

"Ernest."

"I don't know."

"But you had your hand up?"

A kid in the back says, "He was just scratching his head, sir."

Ernest looks quickly round, smiles, and says to the kid,

"Shut up."

I ask, "Didn't you have your hand up?"

"Sure."

"But you don't know the answer?"

"Right."

"Then why did you raise your hand?"

"My mama says it's important to talk a lot in class. She went to law school. She says I should talk a lot."

"And, what," I ask, "are you going to talk about when you raise your hand and don't know the answer?"

"I know lots of answers."

"The answer to *this* question?"

"Which one?"

"You forgot, Ernest?"

"Well, we've been talking a lot," says Ernest.

He gets his laugh from the class.

I say slowly, "The word *desks* ends in a plural *s*."

"Not always, sir."

"No. Not always. But right here, on the board, the way I wrote it, it ends in a plural *s*."

"Because you're talking about several desks."

"You got it."

"So?" The so means why didn't I realize he had it all along.

"There's more, Ernest."

"Go ahead."

That stops me in my tracks for a moment. He's got style, this Ernest. "Fine. Now if the desks own something, all of the desks, not just one, how will you make it possessive?"

"...I didn't raise my hand this time."

"No, I know you didn't. But I am asking you."

"Can you put it in a sentence?"

"Okay, Ernest. The desks'—ah—"

"See, it's hard to do."

"Give me a minute, okay? The desks' blotters... That's it. The desks' blotters!"

"Is that a sentence?"

"Yes! I mean, no. The desks' blotters are soiled."

"I don't know what you're talking about."

The class laughs.

"Blotters, Ernest. Those green things you put on top of desks to absorb spilt ink."

"You got one of those?"

"I used to, Ernest."

"It sounds weird."

"Fine. But how do you spell *desks'*?"

"You just add the apostrophe because you never add an apostrophe plus a possessive *s* when the word already ends in the plural *s*."

"How did you know that?"

"You taught me."

"I mean, before you didn't know it."

"Before when I raised my hand?"

"Yes."

"I didn't understand the question."

"What made you understand it now?"

"I guess I'm smart."

From the side of the room, Eugene says, "Way to go, Ernest!" And they all give him a round of applause.

Does Ernest look round and smile?

Not Ernest.

He gives them the finger.

 Faculty

I'm talking to an evaluator in the coffee room. He and three other fellows have come as a team to write up a report of our school. They will spend three days at it. Once every five or six years it occurs.

Mr. Mumfrey is disarming. He gives the impression of being

in his slippers, smoking his pipe and reading Thackeray.

We are alone, seated across the table from each other. I've just asked him if he's evaluated schools before.

"Oh, yes," he answers.

"Then what is our outstanding characteristic?"

"The way you all love the school."

"You mean, think highly of it."

"Yes."

"We're notoriously smug."

"Maybe not. I wonder if you'd all agree why the school is special. What would you say is its strongest point?"

Mr. Mumfrey is adept.

He is also genuine.

Hell, I tell myself, give it a go.

"We tell the trustees it's us, the faculty. We do it subtly, of course. But that's not our secret. We turn out bright scholars because we take in bright kids. That's the center of it."

"What else?"

"Small classes. That says it all. Twenty bright boys."

"And the faculty is just average?"

"No. I really don't think so."

"Special?"

"Some."

"Why? Why are those especially good? What do they do differently?"

I figure I'm into it now.

I reach over and grab an orange and start peeling it. I like his questions.

"It's who they are. Unusual ducks. Ducks who were flying somewhere else and—"

"Couldn't make it?"

"Perhaps. Or made it and found out once they were there

that it wasn't what they expected. We have a successful ex-stockbroker on the faculty. He's now an excellent teacher. Another colleague was formerly in publishing; one was in advertising; one was an actor. All of them are superior teachers."

"They entered sideways."

"That's exactly it, Mr. Mumfrey."

"And they don't tend to be disgruntled? They're not doing something they'd rather not?"

I take a minute.

"Some teachers are disgruntled. You're right about that. And probably disgruntled because they'd rather not be teaching. Others, though, enter sideways and discover they enjoy spending their days with the children. An unexpected joy. Whether they still have their former ambition or not, they now have a new one—to do right by the child."

"Meanwhile, they have this additional texture, this other background."

"More coffee?" I ask.

"Just a bit."

As I pour, he continues.

"And those who train to be teachers? The direct entrance?"

"Some of those are great. Some aren't. What I'm saying is no school should pass up a good duck. Even if he doesn't have educational credentials."

"What would the criteria be?"

"A degree, and the headmaster's okay. If the headmaster's discernment is off, there's no chance for the school anyway."

"Where does one find this type?"

"Friends, parents, alumni. They know of a young woman. 'Go get her,' they say. 'She's in fashion and hates it!' Dr. Westgate seems to come upon them while vacationing in England. Must be a lot of ducks in Cambridge. But they needn't be English. Just someone who comes to work on time and enjoys the company of children. If he has clear explanations in one pocket and a good nature in the other, don't ask for anything more."

"How do you tell who has a good nature?"

"By looking for a good nature rather than credentials. The headmaster can tell. Be sure you have the right headmaster."

He says nothing.

I ask, "Do I sound smug?"

"Not to listen to. I just wonder how it will read."

 ## A Gentleman

It is time for the class to go to the art room. I watch them as they file through the few feet of hallway and turn into the capable hands of Mr. Bechlof.

Stanley is the last in line. He's in the dumps. I reach out for his hand and say, "Stanley, wait. Come on into the room for a minute."

"I'll be late for art, sir."

"Just for a minute."

Shyly he enters the room.

"Sit, Stanley, sit a minute."

He wants to flee but he obediently does as I ask. "You know, Stanley, the boys weren't laughing at you."

His face turns red.

I know this talk is embarrassing him. He is an extremely private child. I force myself to continue. "I think you're gonna be a great mathematician."

He's surprised.

"You don't agree?" I say.

For a moment he forgets his shyness. "I get all the answers wrong." He can't believe I praised him in math. "I've never been good in math."

"I know. I think that's because you're really bright."

That's too much for Stanley to hear. He's shy once again. "You see," I continue, "you can't memorize very well, and what you do memorize you tend to forget, but you reason beautifully. Do you know what I mean? The thinking part of math, the reasoning part, you do as well as anyone. But between what you forget and your shyness when you speak, you come out with crazy answers and you speak them in a timid voice and that makes the class laugh before I can stop them. Sometimes I laugh myself."

"I don't mind," he says.

"But you do, Stanley."

"I mean when you laugh."

"Ah, because you know I like you." He doesn't answer but he can't quite hide that he's pleased. "Well, I know the class likes you, too."

"They think I'm dumb. They always have."

"You can't blame them for that."

He looks up at me with clouded eyes. "I mean," I say, "you can't blame them for seeing you as you see yourself." He's not shy now. He's not embarrassed. He is totally attentive. He wants very much to understand what I'm saying. He can't afford shyness. "You think you're dumb, Stanley, and that's the big mistake you're making. Your problem is you are gentle. You are a young gentleman, Stanley, and that's a rare commodity in any fourth grade."

He's trying hard to follow.

"You know what a rowdy is?"

He shakes his head no.

"It's a kid who likes to mix it up. Like Jack, like most of the boys in class. It's a young-kid thing that makes them pull pranks and push each other and fuss and laugh. Most of the kids in fourth grade have a lot of that quality. The ones that don't, pretend to have it because they like it in the other boys."

36

"I like it, too."

"So do I. But you don't have it, and it has never occurred to you to pretend to have it, and I don't think you should. You are very much yourself. You're a gentleman, a refined, well-mannered, introspective—I mean thoughtful—rare, young man. I like you for it. And so do the boys. They like you. The thing is, the code of ethics for baseball-playing nine-year-olds is to not show they like it. They've been brainwashed by our society. Their heroes are in the NFL and the American League. It's okay. They'll balance out. And when they are full grown, many of them will be gentlemen and they will also be your friends."

I don't know how much he's gotten but he has been captured. He's forgotten all about himself. "Stanley, take my word on it. It may happen tomorrow or next week or not until the sixth grade, but you're gonna be a top math student and the King of the Hill."

Now we sit like two dummies. He doesn't know what to do and I don't know what to do. We both feel terrific but I've become as shy as he. I notice the snack bag in the back of the room. "You want an apple?" "No, sir." "Better go to art."

The Unique

I'm sure there is a particular factory in heaven that specializes in making diversions for a weary world.

That's where Theo was assembled.

He looks like John Gielgud must have looked at nine years old. He's gaunt, pinched, and he has an astounding nose. A glorious, full-bodied, arresting nose.

Theo rivets you with his close-set eyes and then fixes you with his nose.

In one chain of events I have seen Theo lose his pencil; stand up to complain when he shouldn't; sit down, when told to, at the wrong desk; turn it upside down looking for the pencil; cut his finger packing it back together; rip his pants on the way to show the nurse his cut finger, and lose his glasses on the way back.

To compound his uniqueness, he remains undaunted.
He is aware at each step of the way that extraordinary things are taking place, but instead of it depressing him, each fills him with renewed wonder at the various ways of the gods.
He constantly looks over to me with the roundest, most close-set eyes that say, "I hope you're not missing any of this, Baz. It's unreal."

His associate, Dugan, completes the scene.
Wherever Theo ventures, Dugan trails along. Dugan comes from the same factory, I know it. The day they were assembled the angels were discussing Don Quixote.

Pleasing Words

I've come upon a new and astounding technique. It goes like this:
I'm breaking my back trying to teach Clifford how to do long division. He's having none of it. For some reason he can't pay attention. How can he do that to me, I think. I'm knocking myself out and he is not only not learning, he's unaware of how hard I'm trying.

Then the idea comes to me.

I say, "Clifford, stand up."

He doesn't like the idea.

"Please," I say.

He looks around suspiciously and then says casually, "Sure," and stands.

"Repeat after me, Clifford, okay?"

"Sure."

"Everything I say, you say."

"Okay," Clifford agrees.

He thinks I'm going to go through the steps of doing long division. He figures he'll repeat them, let them go into one of his ears and out the other, and learn them when he's good and ready.

But I say, "Say this, Clifford: 'Mr. Bazarini, Baz-baby,' " and I get a good laugh from the class.

Clifford's unsure.

The class is jolly.

"Go on, Clifford," I urge, "say it."

Clifford ducks his chin momentarily and says, "Mr. Bazarini, Baz-baby!" and gets a better laugh than I did.

"Terrific," I say. "Okay, here's more:

'I just want to tell you—' "

He says, "I just want to tell you—"

Me: "How *much* I appreciate—"

Him: "How much I appreciate—"

Me: "What you're trying to do here."

Him: "What you're trying to do here."

Me: "You are knocking yourself out to teach me."

Him: "You are *really* knocking yourself out to teach me."

He's into it.

The class loves it.

Me: "And it isn't going unnoticed."

Him: "And it isn't going unnoticed *one bit!*"

Yeah!
Laughter.

Me: "You're a great guy, Bazzy!"
Him: "You're a great guy, Baz-baby!"
Me: "And I love you!"
That's too much.
He reddens and sits down to a good round of applause.

 # Happy Home

All of the class is off to Phys. Ed. except Mitchell. He is in the classroom with me. He's been out sick for three days and claims he's still not well enough to play sports.
I ask, "What does your mother do, Mitchell?"
"She's a painter."
"An artist?"
"Yes, sir."
I'm correcting compositions and he is working on a graphic for his Math Project.
"Mitchell, why do you stay home so much?"
"You mean when I'm sick?"
"You don't look to me as if you get sick so much. I'm not mad. I'm trying to understand."
"I have asthma."
"I know."
"My mother thinks it's not good to go outside when it's acting up."
"I think you like to stay home with your mother and paint. Is that what you do?"
"I sometimes read, but mostly, yeah, we paint together."
"I also think your mother likes to have you home. It's great that you both feel that way but you can't miss so much

school. It's a lot of fun, I'm sure."

"Yeah, it's okay."

"But you're not learning all you should. Your mother's gonna have to give you up. Do you know that if you were in public school they'd be very upset?"

"Why?"

"Because how much money a public school gets depends on their attendance. If the kids don't come to school regularly, they don't get as much money."

"She's painting a picture the size of the blackboard."

"Your mom?"

"Yeah. It's got giraffes in it and people dressed up. Ties and hats and umbrellas. It's neat."

"I bet it is."

"She says they ran away from their house to live with the giraffes. I'm making a picture of the house they left. All surrounded by trees, and lonely."

"Beats the metric system, doesn't it?"

 ## Sex and Drugs

Sex and fourth-graders. Of twenty fourth-graders, eighteen are interested in sex. Of the two remaining, one doesn't seem to know it exists and the other would rather not talk about it.

Should I talk about it?

I ask the parents every year. Every October all of the parents are invited to school for drinks, a few remarks from the headmaster, and a visit to the teacher's room. There I tell them what to expect during the school year. Then I ask them. "It comes up," I explain, "usually during reading class. I'm not particularly good at talking about it. On the other hand, it isn't a good idea to sidestep the issue. If any of you object to my going into it, you can tell me now or tell me privately. If one of you objects, I won't do it."

"May I ask what you mean by talking about sex?" This is said by a mother. The other mothers and fathers present accept it as a proper request.

"Yes. Thanks." I take a breath. "It usually begins with procreation. They know mothers carry babies in their stomachs, but about half aren't quite sure how the baby gets there. I tell them how. I explain the physical act of intercourse. One or two of your sons blanch but no one has passed out yet. I explain it simply, honestly, and quickly. But then, I must admit, I can't leave it at that. I can't because I know almost all of them look into those popular magazines devoted to nude ladies. So I go on to talk, simply and quickly, about the pleasure one feels and how that feeling tends to make men think of women as objects."

"They understand that?" a father asks.

"Yes. I talk about how, ideally, there is more to it than that. There is love and affection and consideration and caring. That sex should not be thought of as a plaything. That it should be part of a richer alliance. I put it in different words, and yes, they seem to understand that."

No parent has ever come to me to object.

People do come in from the outside to talk about sex to the boys on a regular basis. That begins in the fifth grade. That's fine, I suppose.

It's just a bit clinical.

I do think it's wrong for those girly magazines to teach the kids that sex is how we use each other for pleasure; but on the other hand, I don't like the romance taken out of it by a clinical approach.

Can someone come in and talk romance?

That's asking for too much, I know.

I have talked about love to my fourth-graders. It is never planned, but it happens.

I tell them, "One day you will look at a girl and feel the

wonder of falling in love. And there is more to it than what you feel looking at a centerfold."

"How can you tell?" a boy asks.

"Tell what?"

"If you're really in love? If this is the girl you should ask to marry you?"

"That's a good question," I say. I remember puzzling that one through as a young man. "There is one thing. I think. At least there was one thought that made me feel certain when I met my wife."

"What was that?"

"For the first time, I was putting someone before myself. Do you know what I mean?"

"Good manners?"

"More than that. Not just doing the proper thing because you know that is what is expected. I mean really preferring to do what she wants rather than what you want. Preferring it because she wants it."

"Then it becomes the thing you want, sir."

"I suppose."

"So you're really doing what you want anyway."

"It ends up that way, doesn't it?" I say.

"So," says another kid, "it's not so bad putting her first."

"Not bad at all," I say. "And if she's doing the same thing, if she's thinking of you first, well, then you're into something marvelous, something ever more important than centerfolds."

A boy in the corner is puzzled.

"You mean, you must always put the girl first?"

"No," I say. "Not at all. Consideration for another is magical stuff. A little of it works magic. I think because it's so rare to come upon. No, you can still think of yourself, take care of yourself, please yourself. That part's all right. I suppose what I mean is when you really fall in love you feel that person becomes a part of you—to consider her is to consider yourself."

A kid says, "Sounds tricky."

Drugs?

Kids must be warned but not alarmed. A delicate balance is called for with the young. We must find ways to gradually introduce them to the pitfalls of the world without painting a world made of pitfalls.

Fourth grade may be the time to begin.

They're so impressionable. I remember coming into a room after a class of mine had been discussing in science the effects of erosion. They were a glum group of kids.

I found out it was the erosion talk. They were all imagining the world eroding each second from under their feet.

Like an ass, the only thing I could think to talk about by way of balance and renewal was new mountain ranges that surge up from beneath us.

That finished them off.

Pitfalls and blazing lava! When they were taking their baths, the tub would either sink beneath them or molten rock would pour in through the window!

Have any of my fourth-graders taken drugs?

Not that I know of.

Should one watch a child that young?

I think so.

Watch for what?

I'd watch for sadness.

Some kids carry sadness around like a constant toothache. Imagine a tooth aching month after month after month and some friend comes along with a pill and says this will make it go away. That would be hard to pass up.

Generally, people with hope are people who stay pure. It's a feeling they seem to have inside of getting stronger, getting better, getting brighter each day. It is a sense of "bettering." Whoever has that feeling within him, that person has patience, that person can endure a setback because he believes in his direction. He feels he is on the right road.

A depressed kid is wandering and frightened.

What depresses them?
What can we do?
As adults, if we're drinking too much, we can stop. If we're getting into debt, we can stop. Kids know when the family's getting into trouble. They know when the supports are rotting.

As adults we have to support those kids we brought into the world. We have to curtail our ambitions if they begin to shake apart the family scene. And we can't expect too much, especially too much too soon. And we can't pick on our kids because we're disappointed in ourselves.

We have to figure out why some kids will do anything to be accepted by their peers. It is a most important area and one that completely mystifies me because I can never remember feeling peer pressure. Not for a moment. When I was sixteen I recall walking home from a dance with five of my friends, all boys, all around sixteen. We were on what used to be called Basin Street in New Orleans. It was about eleven at night and the street was deserted and dark. One of the gang, a fellow called Eddie, said, "Let's steal this car and go for a ride around Lake Ponchartrain." The others started to snicker and give it their thought. I didn't hesitate. I said, "Good night, fellows. See you tomorrow." I didn't pause to explain myself, I didn't try to argue with them, I simply knew I didn't want to get into that and I didn't care what they thought about me. I kept walking home.

And no one tried to argue with me except for a "Hey, Baz, come on, man."

I didn't even turn round.

I was gone.

The next day?

No trouble. No one teased me. I had the same standing with them I had before—not Top Gun, no, but a solid member of the gang. I suppose they could sense I didn't need their approval and that's what made them leave me alone—not leave me alone, they didn't even think to bother me.

I know others who, as young people, were impervious to peer pressure. Did we all have something in common? If we did it was probably confidence in ourselves.

Not that I was cocksure.

But I was confident; I felt I had something to go after and that little by little I was getting closer. It's the feel of your life, the span of it arching into the future, the healthy pull of going for something worthwhile. That "something" could be different things: a career in music, to build a beautiful house, to have children, to be a doctor. A hope. With me, it was an all-encompassing belief in "bettering," a belief in choosing myself better each day.

 ## Half Work

Gaunt Theo is walking beside me as we descend the stairs to lunch.

"Theo," I say, "you're too foolish in class. You should try not to be."

He says, "Sir, you're foolish in class."

"I am?"

"Every day."

"No, Theo."

"Yes. Today you asked Dugan a question and pretended to fall asleep waiting for him to answer."

"That was just to relax Dugan. Make him laugh. Refresh his mind. You see, Theo, when I am foolish, there's a reason."

"Same with me."

"Are you serious?"

"Yes. I try to help break up the day."

"You're good at it."

We reach a stair landing and navigate the turn.
"And, Theo," I say, "you're not doing much work."
He pushes his glasses high up his stately nose and says, "I do my math homework."
"You do half of your math homework."
He ponders.
"Do I have to do it all?"
"It's customary, Theo."
"But all the ones I do I get right."
"That's true, sir," says Dugan. He's somehow worked his way up the line and is right behind us.
"But," I say to Theo, "you do the first half of the problems on the page and they're always the easiest ones. They get harder as they proceed."
Theo says, "Then I'll do the last half."
"He's got a point there, sir. If he does the hard ones perfectly why should he do the easy ones?"
Theo adds, "What's the use of learning?"
I say, "What?"
"I mean, if you learn it, why do you have to keep going over it?"
"For practice, Theo. So you don't forget it."
"But twenty problems are boring. After the tenth problem, I don't care anymore."
"Neither do I," says Dugan.
"But you don't get them right, Dugan!" I say.
"No," he answers, "not every single one."
We enter the straight flight of steps that leads directly to the dining room. I say, "You've got a point, Theo, except the class won't go for it. They'll feel I'm treating you special."
"But I am!"
"He's terrific in math, sir," says Dugan.
I say, "I agree."
Dugan says, "Why don't you tell the other kids if they start doing everything right they'd only have to do the last

half?" Then he looks at Theo and says, "Would you go for that, Theo?"

"Sure."

I yell, "I'm the one who has to go for it, Dugan!"

Dugan answers, "And the class, too, sir. You have to consider them."

Cursing

Though it is only done occasionally, it's traditional to hear a boy deep within a frenzy called an ass. "Charles, don't be an ass!"

The men teachers do it. Short for jackass. But who knows. It certainly gets the attention of a crazed child. It opens his eyes and takes his interest away from whatever action he's committing. It does untold good.

Other than that, not much swearing and cursing go on, though I've been gravely tempted at times both because of provocation and because I know that a cussin' teacher takes on heroic dimensions in the eyes of fourth-graders.

Twice I've been strung out enough by an unending cascade of rascality to mutter, "Shit." Both times it slipped out. And, really, two times in twenty years is the record of a saint.

Once upon a time I used a foul word calmly and deliberately and was given an ovation by the boys. The ovation was spontaneous. And it had nothing to do with the surge of devil-pleasure kids get from seeing an adult let go, succumb, expose, give way. They offered genuine applause. They offered it in appreciation.

I had been explaining during Roman history how Martius, the king, believed the best way to keep peace was to be fully armed. They were intrigued by the idea. Before long we were talking about the arms race with the Russians and that discussion led to talk about the atomic bomb. It wasn't long before they were exposing their fears of a nuclear war. It is quite an experience to see twenty kids courageously show their fears.

They wanted to know everything.

How many people would be killed.

What countries had the bomb.

Who were our enemies.

What would it feel like.

And, finally, when it would happen. As soon as that question was asked by one boy, another boy said, "My bus driver told me that in a year or two they'll drop the atomic bomb here and we'll all die."

A hush followed his statement and in that hush I said, "Any adult that says that to a child is an asshole."

Twenty faces lit with the light of joy. They flushed with happiness for having heard it said. I said it before I could think. I was so upset. But I said it simply and they didn't giggle at the forbidden word. Instead, they applauded the sentiment. They applauded spontaneously and seriously. It was meaningful, sedate, full applause and when it died down one child said in a quiet voice, "Yeah, Baz."

For a moment, things had been set right, and they were thankful.

The more a child awakens to the real world, the more he sees to fear. I remember the experience myself. I remember wondering if I would live long enough to get married. I wondered if I'd live long enough to have children. I wondered if I would see places before they were blown up.

In this time of AIDS, terrorism, the proliferation of nuclear weapons, children are dealing with more fears than any children that have come before.

When teachers say kids are fresher than ever, when

parents say kids don't listen as they used to, when studies say there are more teenage suicides, I think all of it is related to the mass of fear a child has to try to live with. They are missing one of the sweetest things life used to offer—a belief in the future. Why should a child take care of his health if he's uncertain whether there will be a healthy place to live in? Why should he believe in saving some of what he earns if he won't be allowed to be around to spend it? Why should he look for long-time commitments when there won't be a long time?

My fourth-graders and I don't get this deeply into fear but I see it beginning as I see them begin to waken.

 Help

Early morning.

Before the boys enter school for the day, I say to my colleague, David Westcott, "David, I have a solution."

We are in the library glancing through the morning papers. David is in his eighth week as acting headmaster.

He has no idea what I'm talking about.

"Swell," he says, "I have thirty-seven problems. I'm sure I can make a match."

"For poor writing."

We've taught together for twenty years. I'm gray and grizzled while David miraculously retains his hair color. He answers:

"Does this mean that at next week's general faculty meeting you intend to stand and tell the other class masters and mistresses how to teach writing?"

"No."

"Good. What's your idea?"

"Remember, years ago, the entire country was alarmed about poor reading scores?"

David holds his ground. Eight weeks of being acting head has taught him to admit nothing. I squint and continue:

"We got a reading specialist."

"Is that what happened?"

"Yes, David. Now the time has come to have a school writing specialist."

He turns to the theater page of *The New York Times* and mumbles, "Have you thought this through?"

"No, I haven't. I have some vague phrases to aim at you."

"Backed with strong impulse."

"Deep concern, David."

With that I fall silent.

David waits for me to continue but I keep my mouth shut. I press my tongue against the back of my front teeth.

"I know your ploys, Ronald. Now you refuse to speak so that I ask a string of questions to draw you out and end up feeling your idea, whatever it is, is as much mine."

"David, poor writing is there. We can't deny it."

"But it is the province of the classroom teacher."

I'm mute.

He says, "It *is* the job of the English teacher."

"David, the problem writer, the child having difficulty with his pen, cannot be helped in the normal course of events by a class teacher because he, the student, needs individual attention the class teacher can't find time to give (or energy to give). The full day, teacher fatigue, disciplining, grading— too many papers to correct. It can't be expected."

He attends.

"Care," he says.

"Yes. It takes care."

"Serenity."

"Yes, it takes serenity. The student must have it, and the teacher must."

"Clear thought."

"Yes, David, clear thought—the next-to-final discipline—to lead to the ultimate discipline of getting clear thought clearly on paper."

It is one minute before 8:30. David rises. In a minute he will be at the front door to shake hands with each boy as he enters, a St. Bernard's tradition. As he leaves he says, "We're talking here about an ultimate goal!" and he makes me laugh.

Noon.

Over the din of lunch, David asks, "Is there no way of changing our haggard, cranky selves into this god you seek?"

"No way. We need a specialist."

David sprinkles what appears to be fine sawdust onto his salad and asks, "Does he see everyone?"

"You mean first-graders and up?"

"Yes."

"No."

"Why not?"

"We should give a boy at least through the fourth grade to sort himself out. About the fifth grade we can distinguish who needs special help. I'm not sure."

"Fifth-graders on up."

"Yes."

He asks, "Where did you get that orange juice?"

"You push into that machine and out it comes."

"New?"

"Yes. You mean the orange-juice machine?"

"Yes."

"Yes."

"One-on-one?"

"Yes. Boy and specialist."

"You love that word."

" 'Specialist'? No, David, I hate it."

"For how long?"

"Thirty, maybe forty minutes."

"And where does this . . . this helper . . . where does he

find the time? I mean from the boy's schedule?"

"Almost anywhere."

"Don't be cavalier."

"Not from reading, writing, and arithmetic, but from anywhere else. It's much more important for a seventh-grader to get a good crack at writing than to be introduced to Roman history. It would be a shame to send a boy off to boarding school without knowing the stunning similarities between Roman mistakes and our mistakes, but not nearly as terrible as sending him off an inadequate writer. French, take him out of French!"

"Don't get heady, Ronald."

He muses.

"One-on-one."

"Yes."

"How do you go about it?"

"I don't know."

"An honest answer is not necessarily a refreshing one."

"We go about it awkwardly the way Picasso went about his first cubist canvas. Ugly and unsure come first."

He wonders, "Do other schools have writing specialists?"

"What does it matter?"

"We should visit more schools."

"Every time I visit a school they spend the day in assembly."

Afternoon.

By chance, David and I are coating up in front of the school. I ask if he's walking home and join him headed downtown on Fifth.

He asks, "Where do we get the money to hire a new man?"

"I don't care," I answer and David thinks aloud:

"I didn't ask that right."

We fall silent half a block.

I ask, "Is that all?"

"All what?"

"All the questions?"

"Oh, no. For example, who *is* a writing helper?"

"That's the best part. Because we just thought of the position that means there aren't educational courses devised yet. He won't be manufactured via course credits."

"You're on dangerous ground."

"I don't like store-bought hair."

In deference to a fast-moving black Corvette, David slows me down with the back of his arm across my chest. He asks, "So we get someone."

"Yes."

"Who?"

"Someone who can sit at ease next to a child and talk bit by bit about clarity, the grace and shine of clear wording. And mechanics, the nuts and bolts. And grammar. Some marvelous literary fellow, slow-pulsed, who can speak of unity and melody and focus. Some patient soul who will, phrase by phrase, sentence by sentence, help the child record his thoughts."

David shakes his head. "Loose, Ronald. Poetic but loose."

"First the dream and then the blueprint."

"Let's talk blueprint."

I take a few moments and then say, "There must first be discussion."

"The idea."

"Yes. Fully discussed."

He asks, "An outline?"

"No. Not much outlining. Not to begin. No. I mean an exploration of an idea. Let's say—marriage. The good points, the bad."

"A kid writing about marriage?"

"Better than summer camp. The crucial point is that the kid must have something to say. That's why writers write. The helper helps the kid explore an idea and in time the child realizes he has *something to say*! That makes a person *want* to write. And the wanting is what gets it going."

"Having opinions and wanting to express them."

"Yes. Why write otherwise?"

"Marriage? Kids?"

"The burden of writing, David, is usually there because the kid has no interest in what he's writing on. I bet three out of four of our kids are close to someone's crumbling marriage. I bet they have questions and fears and maybe insights.

"If you don't want to write, it's too difficult a task to take up. Make him want to get something down and he'll get it down clearly, cleverly, gracefully."

"No assignment."

"None. They do it together. Side by side. Pleasant. They pretend they're in a paneled drawing room overlooking a lawn rolling down to the Thames."

"Where do we find him?"

"I don't know."

"What about you?"

"I'm a nervous wreck. I'm not the right guy."

"Life is accidental. You think I'm the right person to be headmaster?"

"You're acting head."

"That's true. That's true."

I smile.

How lucky it is to have David to explain it all to rather than some lug-brained Australopithecine.

We've arrived at his corner.

"We'll set it up," he says.

"Fine."

He turns east and I continue down Fifth to meet my son at the dentist.

That happened three years ago. Now we are drawing plans for a new floor to be built on the roof. It will include the Study Rooms: a Reading Room, a Mathematics Room, and a Writing Room. These will be the private dens of the helpers.

 # Front Steps

"Boys, Mrs. Gridley will be ten minutes late today. She has to set up some audiovisual equipment for Friday's assembly."

"Tell us a story," says Harold.

"An army story," says Pete.

"No," says Timmy. "Tell us a story about when you were our age."

"Yeah!" say six others. "Come on, sir!"

"Okay. Let me think."

Harold says, "Tell us about the cave again."

Pete says, "We heard that."

Harold says, "So?"

"Will you let me think?" I say.

They simmer down.

Okay. This happened when I was your age. It—it's about the time—well, I don't want to give it away. I was nine years old and it's October.

I'm in front of my house on Ursulines Street when Sonny Greig comes round the corner pulling his red wagon. Sonny's got blue eyes and light brown hair and he looks like a short version of Bing Crosby.

"Give me a ride, Sonny," I say.

"Sure," he answers, ready to play, ready to have as much fun as we can. He's always like this, smiling, happy, sharing his toys with me. Our mothers are good friends.

He pulls me round the block, I pull him round the block,

and then he treats me to a snowball from the Filipino with the pushcart at the corner. I get chocolate syrup on mine and he gets spearmint.

"How can you get spearmint?" I ask.

"I like it," he says.

"It's green!" I say.

"I like green," he says, laughing good-naturedly. He thinks it's funny that I don't want him to like spearmint.

Later, he pulls all of his marbles out of his pockets and counts them, and I sit in his red wagon holding on to the long handle that I've pulled back towards me. By moving it to the left I can make the wheels turn to the right, and vice versa. I'm pretending I'm in an airplane and I'm holding onto the stick. In my head I'm flying through a storm so I make thunder and lightning sounds as I move the handle to one side and then the other.

"You want a push, Ronald?"

He means he will get behind the wagon and push fast, and I'll sit in the wagon and steer with the brought-back handle.

"Yeah!" I say.

And zoom!

Away we go down the concrete sidewalk past all the fronts of the houses until I lose control of the steering and direct us right into Mrs. Vigo's marble steps.

Crash!

The wagon shudders!

And I fall out.

From the wagon to the ground isn't more than a foot and a half but that's all it takes. When I right myself, I say to Sonny, "Look at my arm."

Octobers are warm in New Orleans and I'm wearing a short-sleeved shirt. Sonny looks at my left arm and screams, "Yaaaaggg!" and runs home. No goodbye, nothing, he just hightails it out of there round the corner and out of sight.

I don't blame him.

My left forearm goes straight out from the elbow as it should but, halfway, it makes a right angle hanging toward the ground. It's not kinda broken; both bones are *completely* broken. My hand and wrist and part of my lower arm have nothing to do with the other half near my elbow.

I grab the hanging half and carefully hold it up on a level and walk the half a block home to Mama. She's cleaning house. It's so hot, she's cleaning the house in her slippers and slip. No dress.

When I walk in she's singing "Mexicali Rose" and is sort of dancing as she dusts the white ceramic dogs she bought at Woolworth's.

I say, "Ma, look!" and when she looks I let go and half of my left arm drops.

She screams, "Aiiiiieeeee!" and starts to do side hops in her slip. Her left arm reaches up to heaven and comes down as her right arm goes up and she keeps alternating as she does these side hops.

She runs right past me into the street screaming, "Aiiiiieeeee!"

In the middle of Ursulines Street, in between the street-car tracks, she continues her crazy dance. Now both her arms are waving above her head and she begins a series of knee lifts with her legs.

"Aiiiiieeeee! Aiiiiieeeee!"

I sit on our front steps and watch her.

I place my left arm gently in my lap and watch Josephine do those knee lifts side to side.

Our neighbor, Mr. Gage, a retired mailman, comes onto his front porch with his buddy, Mike. I like Mike. Mike is about fifty years old but he still has his mother wash and starch his handkerchiefs. When Mike pulls out one of those handkerchiefs to blow his nose, it's a sketch.

58

"Jesus!" says Mr. Gage. "Josephine's lost her mind. Grab her, Mike!"

They grab my mom and throw her into Mr. Gage's four-door DeSoto parked in front of our house. The idea is to take her to the hospital. But in the back seat she yells, "Ronald! It's Ronald!"

Mr. Gage has just started the car.

He looks out at me as he says, "Ronald?"

I hold up my left arm straight and then drop the bottom half.

"Jesus Christ!" says Mr. Gage. "Mike, it's Ronald!"

Mike, seated next to Mr. Gage, looks at me but won't come near my left arm. He looks and not quite looks.

"Ronald, get in here!" says Mr. Gage.

"All right," I say but it's hard for me to open the door until Mike reaches out his hand and does it for me. "Thanks," I say.

Now Mike gets out of the car, slams the door shut and gets back in the front seat with Mr. Gage.

I sit next to my Mom who's leaning back like she's taking a rest but is breathing differently.

"Okay, Ronald?" asks Mr. Gage.

"One minute." I situate myself, get my arm placed nicely on my left leg and say, "Let's go."

He lets up on the clutch and away we go as I sit petting my Mom with my good right hand.

I say, "It's gonna be okay, Mom."

She mumbles, "Oeee."

"Don't worry."

"Oee."

Perfection

It is early May.
Ralph is working on a page for his Math Project Art Book. The assignment is to make ten drawings or graphics each illustrating a mathematical concept. It is a task I've assigned under the influence of Rudolph Steiner. It was assigned in September to be finished by the end of May.

"Ralph," I say, "you have only three weeks left."
"I know," he says.
"How many sheets have you done?"
"Four."
"All year long you've done four!"
"Sir, I'm doing them real good."
"But you won't meet the deadline."

He puts down his coloring pen. "Wait a minute, Baz. You mean if I don't finish all ten by the end of the month I won't get the Math Project Medal?"
"That's the deal."
"That stinks."
"Ralph, you have to learn to accept a deal and stick by it. You have to learn to hand things in on time."
"Hold on." He gives me a hard look. "Have you seen Charley's project?"
I look over at Charley. He's happy as a lark splashing color on paper every which way. "Yes, Ralph," I say, "I have seen his project."
"He's got nine pages done, right?"
"Right."
"If he finishes on time, and he will, will he get the

medal?"

"Yes."

"But his project is a piece of junk!"

I lower my voice. "It is hasty work, I agree."

"And I take my time on every single sheet. My drawings are beautiful."

He's right. They are.

"They are," I say. "Yours is probably the best."

"But I'm not going to finish in time."

"That's right."

"Because I take the time to make it beautiful."

"I know."

"Sir, that stinks!"

"It does."

We think about it.

"Would you like to work on it at home?"

He cocks his head. "You said we could only work on it at school when we got free time."

"I did. But I'll let you work on it at home."

"Great. But that wouldn't be fair to the others."

"Why not?"

"You got to treat us the same."

"Who says?"

"Everybody." He smiles. "Sir! Everybody knows that. It's got to be fair."

"You think it's fair to expect the same from everybody?"

"Isn't it?"

"Is everybody the same?"

"No."

"So I treat everybody differently. That's what's fair. To treat everybody the way they should be treated no matter if it is different from how anyone else is treated."

"I don't know, sir."

I ask him, "Do you think Charley will mind?"

We look over at Charley. Charley's as happy as a lark.

Ralph smiles. "Charley doesn't care."

"So don't worry about it."

I look up to find our new, Augustan headmaster, Stuart Johnson, standing in the doorway. "Trying for justice, Baz?" he asks, and smiles.

"Ralph doesn't think so," I answer.

Ralph says to Mr. Johnson, "I think Charley's his favorite."

"But," says Mr. Johnson, "he just gave you special permission to work on it at home."

"Yeah, I know," says Ralph, "but I think he's covering up."

George R. Dewey's
Fourth-grade Composition:

Alimony

Alimony is money a husband pays a wife if they decide to divorce. In olden days, a husband was given land or money or some big present by the bride's father when the couple were married. If they divorced, the bride didn't get it back. She couldn't live without money; that's why there weren't many divorces.

A husband now pays something to help his wife when they divorce. Husbands don't like to pay alimony, and now that women work, they don't need alimony as much. Sometimes, when a wife has more money, she has to pay alimony to her husband. Wives don't like to pay alimony either.

Maybe children should get alimony. They would have fun with that money. Fathers and mothers should agree to this before divorcing. They should sign a paper, stating clearly that the children should receive all the money. Maybe they would stop fighting and not get a divorce if the money was going to be spent on toys and candy.

Dilemma

How best to teach the children? This quickly becomes: how best to *treat* the children?

A teacher of the young needn't be as expert within an academic discipline as his colleague who teaches university students, but he does have an additional chore. Adults, for the most part, are in class because they wish to endeavor; that all-important act of volition has already been committed. Not children. Children must be taught to want to learn before they can be taught. And that is the dilemma.

If a child is to want to embrace industry, to give his full attention, to put aside baseball fantasies long enough to understand the algorithm of long division and retain it, he must be persuaded within an atmosphere of good cheer like the warm fellowship of trusting partners pledged to search together for the Holy Grail.

The problem is that children are anxious, fearful, and overexcited at times. Some are rambunctious, rebellious, inconsiderate, and astoundingly ill-mannered. Some. At times. There are a few saints, and to those I give my adoration. Here I'm concerned about being fair to those who aren't saints.

Discipline must be maintained. Wrong must be pointed out. Manners must be formed. But if a child is too harshly disciplined, you lose him; he retreats from you for a day, a week, a term. Then you, the teacher, can't achieve your primary task of teaching him. Then you, the parent, are not helping.

Give them freedom, then.

Let them express themselves.

Sounds good, but freedom seems forever to be the right of those already disciplined. The kindest-hearted teacher, often through the practice of his gentle ideas, creates license that leads to chaos. His class becomes unruly and unteachable. The children are not repressed, no, but they become restless.

What is the answer?

The middle ground, of course. The middle, elevated ground.

 # Diversion

We're about to start working on our compositions. The class has just changed out of muddy gym clothes into regular clothes.

Except for Theo.

He has on his new white shirt, his handsome red tie, his brown tweed jacket, but instead of his blue trousers he's wearing his gym sweatpants.

"Theo, what happened?"

"My corduroys are soaking wet, sir."

Standing beside tall, elegant Theo is his stout buddy, Dugan. Dugan says, "They are, sir."

Theo explains, "I sat in the sink."

I inhale calmly and say, "In the sink?"

Theo says, "The sink in the lavatory, yes, sir."

"He did, sir," corroborates Dugan.

I say to Theo, "You went into the lavatory, filled up the sink, and sat in it?"

"Sir!" cries Theo.

Dugan explains, "*I* filled the sink up."

I turn my attention to Dugan. "You filled it up."

"Yes, sir. To wash my hands."

I begin, "Why don't you just—"

"Run the water?" he finishes.

"Yes."

"It seems wasteful."

"I see," I say. "By filling the sink you end with a bowl of dirty water."

Dugan says, "Exactly."

I add, "And there's always the chance Theo might come along and sit in it."

They both laugh.

Theo says, "Sir, I didn't *mean* to sit in it. I was sitting on the edge of the sink and I slipped back. See? Dugan splashed water on the floor—"

"By accident," says Dugan.

"And," continues Theo, "I didn't want to get my new shoes wet and—"

"Slipped back," I say.

"Now you've got it."

"And these sopping corduroy pants?"

"I wrung them out," explains Theo, "and wrapped them in my raincoat."

"Ugh!" says Dugan.

"Good," I say. "Are they in your locker?"

"Of course not," exclaims Theo.

"Your desk?"

"Sir!"

Dugan says, "Geez."

Theo says, "I left them at the front desk for my mother to pick up."

 ## Difficulties

Our receptionist, Flossie Runyon, says, "Burt's mom is upstairs, Baz."

"Oh."

"Didn't you expect her?"

"Yes, I did. I forgot. I'll go right up."

I climb the two flights of stairs slowly, though. Burt's mom is a strong lady. We've talked before. Approach the net and she returns the ball at your head. "How straightforward can I be?"

She's waiting in the empty classroom, standing before my new map, looking down on the Roman Empire.
"Hello," I say.
"Hi. Is this the right time?"
"Oh, yes."
"How long before Burt gets back?"
"We have thirty minutes. Sit."
"Thanks. What are we to do, Mr. Bazarini?"

She's seated behind a boy's desk.
I sit in another boy's chair across from her.

"I don't understand," I say.
"He's doing terribly."
"He's happy. He's getting Bs and Cs."
"But he can do better."
"They can all do better."
"You mean nobody's getting As?"
"I don't mean that. I mean he's preoccupied with his own concerns."
"He's lazy."

She removes her coat.
I say, "He can't stop smiling and joking. He's happy."
"I know. His father and I call him Club Car Harry." She looks straight at me. "But you've got to turn him around."
"I try to. I tell him he's lazy. I tell him not to laugh so much it makes me nervous. I do all those things. He needs more time."
"Time?" she says. "Who has time? When he is ready to

leave here, his record has to get him into Deerfield or his father will be disgraced and his grandfather will have a stroke!"

"You can't insist," I reply.

"Insist! Try it!"

"That's too much like tampering."

"That's setting goals," she says.

"His goals are fine. His rhythm is different from what you'd like."

She's exasperated. "Mr. Bazarini, it is most pleasant to see you in my child's corner, my child's friend, but we want everyone to convince him he must work harder." She is the daughter of a political figure. Her husband is in banking. She likes me but she sees me as a bit too bookish, too content with lack of place.

I read her clearly.

She means me to.

I'm tempted to say to her, "The Chinese consider the highest wisdom accepting a humble position in life." If I do, I know she'll explain, "That's what people in power put forth in order to keep servants at their menial tasks."

"I can't do that," I say.

"You can't?"

"I can persist but I can't insist with a nine-year-old. It's too jarring."

"But you tell me he isn't reading as well as the other children."

"I didn't tell you that."

"You gave him a C."

"He gave himself a C. I recorded it."

"The C compares him to others whether you like it or not."

"It does. I don't like it. I also don't think of him in comparison with others. I think of *him*."

"I want the best for my child."

"I know you do."

"But you disapprove."

"No. I'm just a bit different. I'm telling you to accept difficulty as part of the life of your child. We all have difficulties."

"But it's my job to help my son get rid of his."

"As a father I'm the same way. It's biological. But it's also natural for a woman in labor to push at the wrong time. It's a paradox."

She's trying to see my side but we're nowhere close.

"Your kid makes a lot of jokes," I say, "because he needs a lot of jokes in his life. He gets easily discouraged. You don't shake up a kid like that. He's doing well enough. Shake him up and he'll go into a slump."

I pause and she doesn't speak and that give me courage to go on. I say, "If I told you, 'Talk about problems? What about your husband?' you'd probably answer, 'You don't have to tell me. I live with him!' And if I said to you, 'Talk about problems, what about yourself?' you'd say, 'Oh, God, I have them! I do! I do!' But find out your son has a problem and it's the end of the world."

"We want our children perfect," she says.

"I know. And that's insane. I'm telling you that's insane. What's more, we want the world perfect! For our kids? You bet we do. Perfect! The best school, the best teacher, the best aunt and uncle. If you could replace your husband's brother and his wife you'd probably do it tomorrow."

"I'm a good parent," she says.

"I know you are."

"How can I stop worrying?"

"If you really want to help, face the probability that your child's problem is yours. Or was yours. Restless children usually come from restless parents. Unfortunately, restless parents who should recognize this and be more patient with their child are too restless to be much help."

"You said Burt was happy."

"He's happy when he isn't working. He's restless when he has to."

"So I'm to blame?"

"I hate that word. I said recognize yourself, not blame yourself. And don't blame your mom and dad for making you what you are. Forget about blame. Let's assume everybody's doing his best."

She sighs.

"Now," she says, "I feel terrible because I want my kid to get better grades."

"So do I. That's what I do each day. I teach them the way to the answers all day long. I want them all to get better grades. But I have to treat a kid the way I see him. Burt needs a long line."

She seems suddenly so vulnerable.

The trials and tribulations of being a parent, of worrying every day for the rest of your life about your kids.

I tell her, "The only mistake you and I made was to ask for life's biggest luxury. Having kids. It's like owning a country house. What could be nicer. But you pay through the nose for it every day."

Parents are saints.
Saints suffer.

 Sankta Lucia

The last day of school before Hanukkah and Christmas break.

Our little stage is in the small gym. We're all assembled there for the holiday ceremonies. The boys are wearing coats and ties today. They are seated in rows upon the floor, legs crossed, hair combed, glowing faces looking up toward the proscenium.

A prayer has been said, a school song has been sung. They wait eagerly for what comes next—Mrs. Rhodie's First-grade Presentation! They've seen it before. It's done every year because we like it so.

The lights dim.
The empty stage is in shadows.
The audience can barely see one another.
There is a hush.
The teachers standing along back and side walls look at one another and smile. All is in order.
Mr. Austin opens the back door.
Everyone turns around; a soft rustling; gentle murmurs.
From the rear of the audience the wavering light of candles can be seen. Voices are heard. Mrs. Rhodie and fourteen first-graders have begun to sing:

> Natten går tunga fjat
> Runt gård och stuga
> Kring jord som sol Förlät
> Skuggorna ruva

There is no piano.
Voices alone. One flaxen-haired lady crowned with a garland of holly, and fourteen little boys each carrying a burning taper. They are all in long gowns of white. All of the children are barefoot.
They move like new-minted angels slowly through the audience as they continue to sing the Swedish words:

> Då i vårt mörka bus
> Stiger med tända ljus
> Sankta Lucia
> Sankta Lucia

They've reached the stage.
They climb the short flight of steps carefully. Their eyes are on the melting wax. They form a line of purest white across the apr on of the stage. Pretty, blue-eyed Mrs. Rhodie stands behind them, rising up from the center, the green

leaves and red berries of the holly above all. She stands behind them like a celestial shepherdess.

Fourteen boys in white.
Fourteen tapers burning.
One hundred and forty twinkling toes.

Solemnly, they finish their song and one by one they recite a stanza of a poem written in a seminary in lower Manhattan a long time ago:

'Twas the night before Christmas
And all through the house
Not a creature was stirring
Not even a mouse.

Three hundred jacketed boys and a boundary of teachers listen like proper mice. None of us stirs. All of us watch the passing scene, we hear the piping voices, we usher in together the green and red and purest white of holy days.

 ## Teacher Burnout

My younger son, Peer, brings a note home from school. His teacher thinks he's insubordinate.
I ask, "What did you do?"
"Nothing. I didn't do anything—except—"
"What?"
"I disagree with him."
"You mean you tell him he's wrong in front of the class?"
"No, Dad. I've got some manners, you know. But just because he says something, that doesn't mean it's right, does it?"
"No."
"Well, that's it."

My older son, Nick, got into the same trouble. I remember getting into the same trouble myself. The words of my fifth-grade teacher come back to me. "Mrs. Bazarini, why do you send him to school? Keep him home. He doesn't listen to me!" Well, I listened, but I didn't always agree.

And then a miracle happened. At Yale and Stanford they loved me for this trait. They liked people who disagreed. Opinionated and vociferous! They liked it.

But I decide not to share this with my son Peer.

I say to him, "Why don't you tell your teacher, 'Look, I need a bit more time to arrive at my own conclusion on this?' "

"Who talks like that?" he asks.

"I do," I say.

"No, you think like that, here, when it's all over. Me, I'm in the heat of the classroom!"

I try another tack.

"It's tough being a teacher, Peer."

"Look, Mr. Page likes the kids who do as they're told and don't make waves. That's it. That's what he likes and I'm not that. Period."

"That's because teaching is two jobs. The teaching part is glorious, but the job of keeping the class running smoothly, the job of keeping discipline, is horrible."

"So that means you're not supposed to disagree?"

"No."

"If you're imaginative, they call you too loose; if you think, they call you insubordinate."

"And if you're filled with the vigor of life, they call you a pain in the neck."

"Exactly."

# Adult Pride

I'm at the home of my friend Roger.

"You're a teacher," he says. "You know kids. Tell me what's happening. My kids hate me."

His kids are fifteen and sixteen.

"Roger," I say, "I didn't do too well with my own sons at that age."

"I don't understand it," he says. "My wife and I are so neat. And they live like bums. They don't speak clearly; they have no manners. Other people see it too. It's humiliating. What the hell's wrong?"

I know one thing that's wrong.

His pride.

He's thinking more of himself than he is of his kids. If his children are under par, he's thinking, what must people think of me, the father?

I know because I've done it myself. I remember catching myself at it. I feel a physical pain in my breast recalling how intolerant toward my sons this issue of ego made me. I tried to force upon them standards of taste and behavior it had taken me forty years to achieve. And for all I know they may be working on standards of their own that will far surpass mine.

But I can't tell Roger that.

I continue sitting on the lawn chair drinking ginger ale and watching him organize his garage.

"It started in the seventh grade," he says. "They were seized by a form of insanity. And now they're determined to develop habits that will have them self-destruct by the time they're twenty."

He has stopped working, it seems, to talk to the wall. Then he turns to me. "Cleanliness is out. Sleep is unnecessary. School is embarrassing. Taking advice is prehistoric. The only thing that's important to them is knowing a place that sells discount beer. My dimpled babies have become unruly thugs. Why do they do this?"

"It's nature's way," I say.

"To make you hate your parents?"

"Yes."

"Come on, Baz!"

"It is. They're trying to leave the nest and since you've been so good to them all of their lives they have to convince themselves you're terrible so they can pull away."

"But they think everything I say is wrong!"

"Because they have to feel everything they say is right. That gives them the courage to leave."

"That's nature?"

"Yes. As determined as you are to keep them obedient and dependent on your judgment, that's how determined they are to risk all in order to find their own way. They fight it out. They hurt you and your wife so badly that finally you two begin to think maybe it's not a bad idea to have them get the hell out. It's nature's way to make the separating bearable."

"But they're my kids."

"That's what you've got to give up. For the last fifteen years you've been geared to protect these kids. And now you've got to start giving that up."

"But I worry about them."

"Try to keep most of it to yourself."

"I want to help them."

"Do it discreetly. Remember, they have to convince themselves they don't need your help."

He finds a shoebox of baseball cards to organize.

I sit thinking of how to introduce this matter of his pride.

"Kids want life to be fantastic, Roger."

"All of the time," he says with disgust.

"That's right."

"They don't want to hear about hard work, frugality, patience."

"Not even about cleanliness. They won't be told that eighty percent of our lives must be given up to job and sleep and cleaning up."

"That's too damn foolish," he says.

"And it's also courageous."

"Courageous!" He won't have any part of that.

I think of the courage that kids show in daring to seek the brighter light of a candle burning at both ends.

He says, "They have no judgment."

He's right. Adults have the judgment, but in gaining it most adults turn melancholy; reality tends to make them despair. The child wants no part of that. I say to Roger, "Youth needs hope."

"I love those kids," he says.

"I know. But what they see, Roger, is you raging at them, finding fault with them. That's hard to take. Their friends don't find fault with them. Their friends love them. That's the way they see it."

"But kids *do* have faults!"

"They do."

"So?" he says. "Don't parents have to point that out?"

"Yes, but they must try to point it out without sounding unloving."

"But I'm human. I lose control."

"That's the problem. And it's a big problem. That's why we can't afford to worsen it by bringing our own pride and humiliation into play."

"What?"

"We can't be thinking about ourselves and how they embarrass us in front of others."

"I'm too proud?"

"We all are. But we care more for our children than we do

for our pride. So we have to give it up. It's natural to feel that humiliation but it's also primitive and worthless. You give it up and I'll guarantee everybody will breathe more easily."

He says, "You know what I think, Baz?"
"What?"
"I think you've been around kids too long. I mean it. You see everything their way."
"That's nonsense."
"You do."

 ## Manners

We have just begun to read Kipling's *The Jungle Books*. On page one, Clifford takes exception.
"But, sir, this dog Tabaqui is just doing what he has to do."
"Tabaqui is a jackal. *Doglike*."
"Okay. He's hungry, right?"
"Yes, Clifford," I say, "but he's also sniveling."
"Sniveling?"
Ernest says, "That means his nose is dripping."
Clifford stares at Ernest and then asks me, "Is that right, sir?"
I say, "That's not what I meant."
Ernest says, "When I've got a cold and my nose is dripping all over, my mother says, 'Stop sniveling!' "
"Is that true, sir?" asks Clifford.
"Yes," I say, "but I also mean he's pretending to Father Wolf, he's flattering Father Wolf to get what he wants."
"Sure," says Clifford. "He wants to eat!"
Ernest explains to Clifford, "Look, Clifford, sir knows this jackal is hungry, but sir means that's no reason he has to be a nerd."

"Is that true, sir?"

"Yes!" I say. "Thanks, Ernest."

Clifford stares at Ernest in disbelief.

The rest of the class has been watching the three of us.

"Look, sir," says Clifford, "you're always telling us to be cheerful, right? Well, that's what Tabaqui's doing."

"He's being pleasing."

Ernest turns to Clifford. "Look, Clifford, sir means being pleasing and cheerful aren't the same thing."

"I know what sir means, okay!" Clifford declares. "Just butt out, Ernest. I'm trying to say something."

"Clifford," I explain, "when you just try to please people you lose your dignity."

"What does that mean?"

Ernest explains, "That means you can tell your mother you don't have to please her, 'cause sir says it's bad."

Clifford asks, "Is that what it means, sir?"

"No," I say.

He turns to Ernest. "Shut up, Ernest!"

"That's what I thought he meant."

"I mean," I say, "that you shouldn't feel you have to please everybody."

Ernest says, "Just please yourself."

Clifford looks at Ernest and then at me.

I say, "In a way."

"But," says Clifford, "isn't that bad manners?"

I say, "No."

"I don't get it."

Ernest is about to speak.

"Shut up! Alright?" says Clifford.

I explain. "What we have to do is be cheerful to everyone. That's our social duty. Cheerful but not necessarily pleasing. Shallow people are the ones who try to please all the time, people without any belief in themselves. That's it."

I think Clifford gets it.

He's very thoughtful.

The rest of the class is happy. They enjoy listening to Ernest and Clifford converse.

Ernest says, "This business about good manners is screwy."

"What is it?" I ask.

"I can't make out what's right."

"What have you been taught?"

"Well, Mom says when I'm at somebody's house I shouldn't talk about myself all the time."

Clifford adds, "That's true, sir, he always talks about himself."

"At least I don't brag like you."

"Who says?"

"Boys, cut it out. So you don't talk about yourself. What's wrong with that?"

Ernest says, "Well, I don't talk about myself and that makes the kid I'm with talk about himself all day. And when I leave and say to him, boy, you talked about yourself all day, his mother tells me I have bad manners to say that."

"You've got a point," I say. "If by having good manners you allow the other person to indulge in bad manners, you really haven't shown good manners."

Clifford asks Ernest, "Is that what you said?"

Ernest replies, "Uh-huh."

Spirit

Children are born with spirit. They are born with a belief in themselves and a strong will to do as they see fit. It couldn't be more evident than during the Terrible Twos, in the way those lusty two-year-olds say "NO!"

Should a child be allowed to keep this spirit?
Or should it be crushed?
Or is there a middle, elevated ground?

It's a big decision.

If Mom and Dad decide to crush it, and especially if they act before the kid is six or seven, they will have great success. They can succeed in making their child believe he has no choice but to do as they say. In all things. That child will become the well-behaved child, the prompt child, and maybe even the tidy child. He will be the darling of those teachers who don't like complications. He will receive splendid grades in grammar school. He will, also, not have spirit.

The results will show up later on.

As he enters higher education and deals more with abstract thinking, he may find it difficult to reason on his own. He will not be in the habit of believing in his own feelings and opinions and insights. It will not be part of his nature to mix and relate them and offer his own thought as a unique contribution. He will have been taught not to be unique. He will have been taught to stay in place, to blend, to agree, and to please. Many feel unique is too close to weird. But unique like Edison is not weird; unique like Lincoln, like Bill Cosby, like your favorite aunt, like Babe Ruth is not weird. Your favorite friends? They're the ones full of spirit.

"Hold on, Mr. Teacher! I want my son to rise in the corporate world!"

How high?

Notice who sits at the top of the corporate world. They're unique.

Pressing

It is 11:20 a.m. The children have just left for Phys. Ed. Billy's mother arrives for our conference, a conference she asked for.

"Hello, Mr. Bazarini."

"Hi. Hi. Sit down. Here. Have a seat."

She is pretty and young and uneasy. I have no idea why she has come to see me.

"I don't mean to stay long. I'm sure you have a lot to do."

It sounds bad to me. Now I have an inkling.

"What is it? Tell me what's on your mind. My goodness, don't be upset."

"Billy likes you so much."

"It's as bad as that, huh?"

She smiles. "He does. For the first few months of this year I've never seen him leave for school so happy."

"It's the fourth grade. It's being nine and learning how to hit homers. But he isn't happy now?"

"Haven't you noticed?"

"No."

"Oh."

"But," I say, "that's not unusual. There's something I do wrong, something about me. The kids don't show me their troubles." Though I like her, I'm uneasy now, myself, and it makes me loquacious. "I don't understand it. It's as if I indicate I don't want to hear about their woes."

"I think it's because you're the first man teacher they have, and they try to be manly."

"How sweet of you. Now, that could be. But, no, he hasn't shown me anything."

She's still trying to hold back.

I encourage her. "What is it?"

"At home, these past few weeks, he's been impossible. He's upset all the time, he yells at me, he's picking on his little sister."

"And you think it's something happening at school?"

"He frets over his homework. He says you think he is dumb."

"I don't."

"Oh, I know that. And he does. It's just that he wants you to think he's terrific."

"What can we do?"

"Oh, I didn't come with any answers." She is smiling the smile of a mother who loves her child.

"I think I know what it is."

"I'm sure you're not doing anything wrong, it's just—"

"I am doing something wrong. I'm pretty sure. And I can correct it."

"You can?"

"Today. And by tomorrow you'll see a difference."

She's laughing now. "What is it, Mr Bazarini?"

"Another fault of mine. A trap I know about but I keep falling into. And it happens every year, I'm ashamed to say. Every year there is a kid who comes right to the verge of a breakthrough. With Billy it's math. He is just about to understand it all. I sense it in my bones. I've watched him throughout the year get closer and closer and happier and happier. But when he gets right there, when he has to take only one more step, get into the habit of using just this much more vigor, when he gets that close I lose control and begin to pounce."

I pause and then continue. "I get so charged. I want to lift the kid up and throw him over the last hurdle and shout hurrahs like a victor possessed. I want so much for him to make that last thrilling step that I lose track of the kid, I mean of his feelings. I stay on his case through most of the class. I begin to insist. I'm having the time of my life, but the kid starts to fret. He wants so much to please me but all he sees is a maniac who won't stop urging him to leap. It gets him crazy. And he keeps it to himself until he gets home where he can take it out on his one sure bet, mother."

Her manners are good. She sits silently.

I say, "That's it!"

"It could be."

"It is. I'm sure."

"I think you're right. And you can stop?"

"Stop? Of course. I'll stop today. I *see* it now. The rest will be easy."

Scholarship

Gaunt Theo and faithful Dugan are in the hallway. They've devised a game in which Dugan means to pick up Theo and throw him gracefully into Teddy's locker.

I say to them, "Why aren't you at music?"

Dugan answers with an air of conviction. "Mr. Morris threw Theo out of class."

Theo verifies Dugan's statement with a solemn nod.

I say, "And, you, Dugan, decided to tag along."

Theo senses Dugan will have trouble with that one, so he takes over.

Theo says, "Mr. Morris said I was wasting my parents' money because I wasn't learning everything." He takes his glasses off his formidable nose, looks at me cross-eyed, and continues, "So I asked him, 'What if you were here on half-scholarship? Would that mean you'd only have to learn half?' "

Dugan likes the turn of the conversation. He jumps back in. "So I asked him, what about a kid on full scholarship?" I fill in.

"Meaning that kid wouldn't have to learn anything."

Dugan says, "That's what I told him."

He and Theo are proud of me, the way I follow their talk.

Theo philosophizes, "I mean, it isn't Mr. Morris's money we're wasting."

I ask, "You told him that?"

Theo asks, "Should I?"

I say, "Next time."

 ## Gentle Persistence

We're into the new school year.

It's become our habit to end poetry class with someone reciting his favorite poem. Then a day comes when no one has a poem to offer, so I say:

"I'll recite *my* favorite poem. An anonymous poem."

A boy asks, "What kind of poem is that?"

"Anonymous—it means we don't know who wrote it."

"How come?"

"Well, we know it's from a writer who lived in Lancashire, England, or thereabouts, but maybe he never wrote it down. Maybe a woman wrote it. It was probably just recited aloud for years, and by the time someone wrote it down no one remembered who wrote it."

"Well, can't they find out?"

"Thomas," I say, "will you let me recite the poem?"

"Sure."

"Be quiet, Thomas," says Craig.

"Thanks, Craig," I say.

"Go on, sir," he answers.

"Now, remember," I say, "if you start to fidget I'm stopping. I'm not going to ruin my favorite poem by reading it to crackling paper, coughs, and shuffling feet. Okay."
I take up a slim book on poetry and find it.
I read:

> As I was going down Treak Street
> For half a pound of treacle,

"What's treacle, sir?"
"Will you be quiet, Andrew?" I say.
"All right. All right."
"It's like a sweet, a candy. Comes from molasses, I think."
"All right."

I continue:

> Who should I meet but my old friend Micky Thumps.
> He said to me, "Wilt thou come to our wake?"
> I thought a bit,
> I thought a bit,
> I said I didn't mind:
> So I went.
>
> As I was sitting on our doorstep
> Who should come by but my old friend
> Micky Thumps' brother.
> He said to me, "Wilt thou come to our house?
> Micky is ill."
> I thought a bit,
> I thought a bit,
> I said I didn't mind:
> So I went.
>
> And he were ill:
> He were gravely ill.
> He said to me,
> "Wilt thou come to my funeral, mon, if I die?"
> I thought a bit,
> I thought a bit,

84

I said I didn't mind:
So I went.

And it *were* a funeral.
Some stamped on his grave:
Some spat on his grave:
But I scraped my eyes out for my old friend
  Micky Thumps.

They began being eager to hear my favorite poem but by the second stanza they were indeed fidgeting. By the third, they lost interest.

I carried on, finished, and made no comment about anything, poem or reception.

Weeks later, I close the poetry class reciting the same poem. When they realize it's the one I had said before, they look glum.

"That's a sad poem, sir," says Thomas.

"I know," I say. "We can't have jokes all the time."

Three weeks later I do it again.

Andrew says, "Oh, sir, not again!"

And through the year I recite it four or five times more despite their protestations and without any counterprotestations of my own. I never tell them they should like the poem. I read it and go on to something else.

March comes.
I read it again.
This time they listen.
They don't squirm and rustle about.
They listen seriously.
The week before school ends, I begin:

  As I was going down Treak Street
  For half a pound of treacle,

When I say, "Half a pound of treacle," two boys say it

with me. Six boys start the next line with me. Without bidding or encouragement, they join in. We end the first stanza, all saying it together. And they are solemnly enjoying it the way I have always enjoyed it. More, they are unaware. They say the rest of the poem with me unaware. We finish together and say nothing about it or about reciting it together.

The last day of school is really a half-day, the three morning hours before noon dismissal and summer vacation. I spend these hours doing whatever the boys want: we tell about exciting things that have happened to us; I explain how to make a rubber and china-ball gun; we perform magic tricks; we sing funny songs and the like. But with a half-hour to go to summer freedom, when I ask, "What would you like to do next," a boy answers, "Recite us your poem, sir." And the others say, "Yes, Micky Thumps." And I say, "I will. I will."

 ## Writers

Most everyone has gone home. Barry's mother is going to be late. He decides to wait for her upstairs with me. I'm making notes from Durant for my Roman history course.

"Sir?"

"Yes?"

I answer but I keep working. It is quiet in the room. The late afternoon sun has flooded my desk.

"Is it true you write plays for Broadway?"

I think a bit.

"Yes, I write plays I hope will be done on Broadway."

"That's what I thought. My father says you've been trying to write plays all of your life."

"Your father's right. That's true. How does he know that?"

"I don't know. Is it hard?"

"To write plays? Yes. It is terribly hard. They are the hardest thing in the world to write. For me, anyway. Tennessee may have a different story."

"Are you from Tennessee?"

"No. Just a joke."

I go back to note-taking.

"Sir?"

"Yes, Barry."

"Have any of your plays ever been done? I mean can we go see one?"

"Well, a musical I wrote with Corinna, my wife, has been optioned by Mary Tyler Moore Enterprises. If they decide to do it, I'll take you and your father to see it."

"What's it called?"

"Lucky Lucy and the Fortune Man."

"Good title."

"It is, isn't it? And I have a straight play I'm developing at the New York Shakespeare Festival with Bill Hart. That could be done."

"Do you get paid a lot for that?"

"Nothing much to speak of. A play has to be a hit. A musical has to be a hit. Only one out of twenty that are produced are hits and only one out of six hundred are produced in the first place. Odds are twelve thousand to one of making any money."

"Then why do you do it?"

"I'm driven. You see here before you, Barry, a driven man."

"What's that mean?"

"That means I've got to write them whether I like it or not, whether I'm successful or not."

"Everyone wants to be a success."

"I suppose so."

"How long will you keep trying?"

"Until I drop in my tracks. You see, for a long time it got me down, not getting anything produced. But then I realized it was not my job to get my plays produced. That was someone else's job. My job was to write them. To keep writing them and to keep writing them better. That's my job. And I like it."

"Would you like to stop teaching?"

"Barry, old buddy, maybe for a year. That sound terrible? I would like a year alone at my typewriter. I have a play and a book I'd like to get out. But then I'll come back."

"I'll be in the sixth grade."

"We could still have a drink now and then."

"You like to teach?"

"I love it. To teach. I don't like the policework, the nagging, the having to watch you guys every minute of the day to be sure you don't break your necks. And I don't like getting up in the dark on cold February mornings. We should have Februarys off."

"Neat."

"What about you?"

"What?"

"Are you writing anything?"

"Yes, the compo you assigned on Malaria. It's not due till next week."

"I mean anything else?"

"No. I'm not—?"

"Driven."

"Driven. No way."

 Repeating

Sports Day has concluded.

My class has won the baseball game ribbon and the relay ribbon. We were no threat at all in the tug-of-war.

I've accepted an invitation from one of my mothers to stay and share her picnic under the oak trees of Central

Park. Families are scattered all about us in the shade, but we are relatively alone. We sit like two kids crossed-legged on a cotton blanket.

Her son may have to be kept back.

She asks, "Do you make the decision?"

"No. Not alone. The headmaster, the head of the Middle School, his other teachers, we'll all discuss it."

"If you move him up to the fifth grade isn't there a chance he'll improve? He's just immature."

"That could be. The thing is, if holding him back is the right thing to do, then the earlier we do it the more he benefits. Each year he enters a new grade one year more mature. He's half a year younger than most of the class."

"That's really the problem."

I shake my head in agreement and say, "We want to be sure he's ready for the Upper School."

"It gets harder?"

"It's a responsibility they feel, the Upper School faculty. They want to get him into a good boarding school. They feel a pressure fourth-grade teachers don't experience. Parents start to get nervous when their child is in eighth grade and still faltering."

"Prep schools. Is that what it's all about?"

"No. It's about sticking with the kid and doing the best we can to educate him."

"Then they should forget about the pressure of prep schools."

"Some parents don't allow that. Some parents think that because their son goes to school here, he's assured a proper berth at Andover."

She slices the last sandwich in half and we share it.

"Do you think he should be kept back?" I ask.

"I'm trying to decide."

"Let me know. Try to find out how your son feels about it. At first he won't like the idea, but then a kid sometimes indicates he'd appreciate things getting easier."

Best Friend

Theo: Could I move my desk, sir?
Me: Why?
Theo: Away from Dugan. Way away!
Me: Dugan's your best friend.
Theo: You call this a best friend?
(He opens his desk)
Me: What's that?
Theo: Ice cream!
Me: It doesn't look like ice cream.
Theo: Melted ice cream!
Me: Dugan melted ice cream in your desk?
Theo: Right! That's a best friend?

Child Pride

"Michael thinks he's the smartest boy in class."
I'm saying this to his father.
"And he isn't?"
"No."
"You mean he's covering up an inferiority complex?" His father is fair-haired and burly. He's a doctor.
"No," I answer. "I think it's a straightforward superiority complex."
"Which he doesn't deserve."
"More than that. It's getting in his way. He resents me and

he resents the other boys because we don't crown him Emperor."

"He's competitive. The whole family is."

I'm glad to hear him say it.

"He is," I agree. "He doesn't hustle and yet he wants to be the winner. It's unusual. He quietly sits there mad at us all because he's not in the lead."

"The best math student."

"Yes. He thinks he's that."

Dad firms his jaw.

He says, "This is a new development."

He waits to see how I take this.

I say, "Not according to his previous teachers."

Dad is irritated.

"They told you that?"

I take my time to answer.

"I never ask a child's former teachers what he's like until I've had a couple of months to see for myself. I saw this in Michael and then went to see if other teachers could help me understand it."

"How did they explain it?"

"None of them did. But they all agreed that some unusual pride was at work."

Dad thinks. He says, "He can't keep his mind on anything. You have to make him pay attention."

"I'm trying. I try to draw him out in class, try to gently focus on him and make him attend."

"That doesn't work?"

"No. He smiles. Not fresh. He stays within himself, confidently, and smiles."

"Maybe you're too gentle."

"When I insist, he gets angry."

Dad taps his foot.

He says, "I know about that."

We've reached a turning point. He's showing me he sees the same child I do. He knows I'm on his kid's side, that I'm just trying to talk straight.

"Somewhere along the line," I say, "somehow, he has been made to believe that all honors should come to him as a matter of course. Because he is he. It has to do with pride."

"He doesn't think he has to work for it."

"He really doesn't try at all. Or, at least, not very much."

"And the other kids do?"

"Oh, yes. And half of them enjoy it. Do it naturally."

"I admit I do see a proud kid—"

"Pride isn't all bad," I say.

"No. But not this thing Michael has."

"No. Mind you, I don't think of your son as a 'problem' child, but he does have this problem."

"He's gonna have to get himself together, Mr. Bazarini."

"He will."

"When?" And he laughs.

"Tomorrow, could be. It only takes one clear thought to make a kid change. Maybe in college."

"College!"

"College isn't too late. Didn't Einstein get a slow start?" I take a breath. "Maybe he's lazy. This pride may have developed to shake him into action. Could be."

"What do I do to help?"

That's the big question.

Who has the big answer?

I say, "You can't force a kid to change his outlook, his personality, but you can be ready to point out this or that about pride when the time is right. Pick the right spots."

"Keep an eye on him."

"And yourselves. It could be the family. Unknowingly you could be sending him the wrong message."

"Making him smug."

"Could be."

That afternoon during prep period (that's the last period

of the day, a time when the boys can get a start on their homework), I take Michael aside, one-on-one. This is the one time of the day I can help him without him feeling disgraced. The other boys are busy with their assignments. No one is paying attention to us.

I look at what he's done so far.
Six of the twelve fraction-addition problems are wrong. We're adding fractions with unlike denominators. Tricky work. Thoughtful work. We have been with it for two weeks, and for two weeks Michael does one wrong for every one he does right.

Is he guessing?
No. These are problems you cannot guess at and get right. He gets half of them right because he *understands* how to do them. Yet he averages 50 percent.
I point this out to him.
"Michael, it means you don't apply yourself half of the time. Why?"
"I don't know." He's smiling.
He has thick black hair and rough blue eyes. He has a strong nose. Michael is a fierce hombre.
"Here, this one's wrong," I say. "It should be five-twelfths."
"No, it shouldn't," he says. "It's right."
"Wrong," I say.
"I'm sorry, it's right." He's still smiling. He likes confrontations, when nobody is looking. He has got the mask of confidence. And he knows I don't have the killer instinct.
I'm cool.
I go through the steps and he watches.
"You see," I say. "It's five-twelfths."
"Oh, yes. It's five-twelfths."
"Good. Now go do these five over."

I turn back to my work but he doesn't move.
"No," he says, "I've done those problems. I've done my

homework."

"Michael, do them over."

"I won't!" Now he's upset. That quickly.

I back away.

If I insist, I unleash his pride.

Besides, I don't want to win a battle. That's not why I'm here.

What about teaching?

I've taught him.

He knows how to do these problems. There is no doubt of that. There is no doubt, also, that he has balked and I think he has a good reason for it. I don't understand it completely, I'm sure he doesn't. I only understand it's there, the reason. It's there and it makes it impossible for a boy who understands how to do something to do it correctly.

Now is not the time to show him who's boss.

Not this particular child.

It's the time to have patience. He's old enough to have the pride but he may be far too young to puzzle through why it's there and in how many ways it hurts him. I feel anything less than patience would amount to tampering, and it is far more important not to tamper than to insist on a higher percentage of correct answers.

 # The Willing Moment

Math class.

I am not upset.

The class understands that. But they know I'm tense. What I'm about to say is important.

"I just saw it!"

I say it in a low voice. I make it sound as meaningful as I can.

"I see it every day, and *I just saw it!*"

Gingerly they look around to see who did something awful.

"The instant came, and now it is gone!"
Then I fall into a profound silence.

Chester can't take the suspense.
"What happened, sir?"
Chester's not courageous: he simply can't take suspense.
"What happened?" he repeats.

"This is what happened, Chester. I just taught you an idea, the idea that a fraction is like a division problem. That in the fraction fifteen-thirds the numerator fifteen is the dividend and the denominator three is the divisor. Right? Three into fifteen is five. That's what fifteen-thirds equals."
Chester answers for all. "Yes, sir."
"Fine. The instant came when all of you understood that if you divide the bottom number into the top number, you find out what the fraction is worth. I've been preparing you to learn this for the last three math periods. And the instant came, I delivered the punch line, and you all understood!"

"That's the instant, right?" asks Chester.
"No!" I declaim. "The instant is the *next* instant. The Willing Moment! What you do in that moment is crucial!"

Dan asks, "What did we do?"
"Dan, this is what some of you did. Some of you said to yourselves, '*Remember that.*' You willed yourselves to remember what you had just understood. Calmly, you said to yourselves, 'Remember that.' "

Chester says, "I understood it."

"Yes, Chester, you did. But will you understand it tomorrow? Next week? Because some of you didn't experience the Willing Moment. What you guys experienced was something less vigorous. You guys let the knowledge go in and right out again. You understood it but you didn't grab it. You didn't make it yours!"

I pause and then say: "What have I been telling you is the most important thing to do?"

"Think." They all say it.

"Yes. And what is the next important thing?"

No one knows.

Then one boy, Peter, says, "Retain."

"Yes!"

Chester says, "I forgot what that means."

"It means, remember, Chester."

"Oh, yeah."

"If you do, Chester, miracles will happen. You'll learn in a week what you didn't in a semester."

He asks, "But how do you do it?"

"By willing it, Chester. By wanting to be the best guy you can be. Right this minute you can start your life over. You can choose yourself different, better! Do it, Chester! Do it! You'll enjoy yourself."

The act of volition.

What makes some boys will themselves to learn while other boys, just as bright, don't?

With a few it looks most like natural curiosity.

With some it's material wealth. I've seen fourth-graders connect doing well in school with growing up to own season passes to the Giant games.

Sometimes a kid wants to be wonderful for somebody— his mother, his older brother.

A few get religion, or philosophy, or something else deep and mystifying.

The first step is the hardest.

After that, once they will it, the rewards are so evident, the child begins to thrill. That first grammar test he passes on his own without tearful study sessions at home is a milestone. He feels grand.

He has to do it himself, though. He can't be forced.

Boswell's father didn't approve of him. Boswell complained of it to Sam Johnson. He told Johnson that his father faulted him at every turn. Johnson explained to Boswell that his father expected him to be at twenty what he would be like at thirty.

I have paraphrased and Johnson may have exaggerated, but there is a truth here. Children need time, and they need parents who believe in them.

The voluntary power.

It's worth trying to uncork.

Will.

Volition.

Volo:fly!

The urge to fly comes when it comes. We don't own the child; the child owns himself. We watch over him until he can safely fly on his own.

Apperception.

Perception in which the mind is conscious of the act of perceiving. It's being conscious of the fact that we can choose to be conscious.

Boredom

Paul's mother is dark-haired and hazel-eyed. She is strikingly handsome, someone you would expect to find in a mystery set in Algiers.

We're holding the conference in a corner of the school dining room while the waitresses are cleaning up. She doesn't like the place, but we've looked high and low and can't find another.

She comes right to the point.

"Paul says he's bored," she explains. " 'I'm bored in school,' he says."

"I know," I say. "He's told me the same thing."

"Do you agree?"

"What do you think he means by bored?"

She takes a breath slowly and then sighs. "Well, I suppose he means class isn't interesting. Excuse me, I'm also assuming we should speak candidly."

"Exactly."

With that I fall silent.

She feels she's been abrupt and has hurt my feelings. I'm trying to find the right words to explain an unusual situation.

"I know he's bright," she says. "Perhaps he's not placed properly. I don't know."

"He is bright," I answer, "but so are the other boys. He falls about the middle of the class. I have no complaints about him."

"Why, then, is he bored?"

"He may not be."

"He's lying?"

"No. He isn't a child that lies. He may think he's bored.

98

He may have convinced himself. Of course, he could be right. He may actually be, in the sense you have defined. He may find the pace of the class, the content, too simple. But I don't think so."

She smiles. "Are you going to say what you think?"

"Oh, yes."

"You're just preparing me cautiously for the kill." It's a statement delivered with another smile. Pure Algerian. It gives me courage, too. Her manner and word indicate she may, in spite of her protectiveness, want to hear the truth. The truth? Well, want to hear what I have to say.

"First," I begin, "life in the classroom is not always sparkle time. Much can be turned into games and humor, much of the teaching can, but some simply takes effort, perseverance, and perspiration. Rather than bored, I think Paul is restless. Remember, now, I find him a good student, well-mannered, and great fun. We're not talking about a complaint of mine. But if you want me to pursue what you've brought up, I will, except to talk about it honestly I have to talk beyond the scope of the classroom. We could stop here."

"Go on."

"I think he's trying to live up to too high a standard. I don't know who makes him feel this way but that's the picture I get. It makes him anxious, restless."

"How does that connect with feeling bored?"

"He has trouble with directions. Most directions are in two or three parts. You have to follow each part carefully to understand the whole. The same is true of classroom-teacher explanations. Explaining something is much like giving the child a direction which will help him learn it."

"I don't understand."

"Paul is bright but, because he's restless, he wants to understand how to do the homework, or understand the new concept being explained, in a leap. All at once. He doesn't want to listen to what *A* means, what *B* means, and then relate them to understand *C*. He wants *C* immediately.

When he doesn't get it immediately, he frets. Now, because he's fretting, he misses the explanation of B and is lost. When we get to C, he doesn't know where we are. But he does know he's bright and he does know he can really understand if all goes well. But it hasn't gone well for him."

"That makes him find it boring?"

"Once he doesn't know what's going on, he's hurt and that makes him stop all thinking and that may make him think he is bored."

"You're saying he feels a need to protect himself."

"Yes, that's what I'm saying."

"He identifies feeling puzzled with being bored."

"That could be it."

"But then how does he learn?"

"I don't know."

"You don't?"

"No, I don't know how Paul learns. He's puzzled, he frets, he's lost, and then a week later he understands it. Of course, like a good teacher, I've been reintroducing the concept every day in different ways. When I do this I see this one pick it up and then that one. Paul? During it all he seems confused, out of it. I see him shaking his head like an old man who can't find any more strength to climb the hill. Then he has it."

"It's a mystery," she says.

Yes, I think to myself, but mystery is nothing new in your life.

Spoiled children often decide they're bored. The child who is pampered and constantly entertained resents when labor is the activity of the moment. Especially if he's bright. "Oh, here comes the part where we have to use our brains. Goodbye." He turns off just as the teacher begins to relate that crucial beginning information. As a result he doesn't enter the search.

 Stealing

Math class has finished early. We have ten minutes before lunch. The boys sit still, they seem to sense what I'm about to bring up.

"We all agree that someone has been stealing money from several of you during the past week. Quite a bit of money."

They dare not move their heads. Most of them are pretty sure who the boy is. Rather than look at him they move their eyes and try to catch the eyes of others who know.

"Theft is bad." I take my time. I want to say this just right. "We all know that. It's bad for the boy who does the stealing and it makes the rest of you unsure of whom to trust. One of the worst things of all is what I'm doing now. The thief has made it necessary for me to talk to all of you about stealing. It makes it look as if I'm suspicious of all of you and I'm not."

"Sir, maybe you could find out who did it?"

"Sir, you could question us."

"No. I've never done that and I'm not going to start now. Some of you are so sensitive that if I holler at the boy next to you, you take it personally. I'm not going to question you."

"Then how will you know?"

"I don't want to know. But I do want to talk to him this way. He hearing and I not knowing. I'll be a preacher but not an investigator. I'm not going to spoil the entire atmosphere of this class."

"How are you gonna make him stop?"

"I lost five dollars."

"He's gotta make himself stop," I say. "That's the only

thing that will work, anyway. The only thing I want is for him to hear what I'm about to say. I want him to know that at the moment he stole the money, he was a thief. When he stole again, he was a thief again. But he can decide right now not to be a thief anymore. He has that open to him. If he does decide that, if he says to himself, right now, I'm not going to steal again, then he is no longer a thief. Even though he stole before, he will never, ever be a thief again. And no one will think of him as one. It's up to him."

Someone says, "If it's who I think it is, I know he didn't need the money."

"Yeah, he's rich."

"He just wanted to see if he could get away with it."

"Everybody used to steal in the first grade."

"Yeah, but we stopped."

And then, "Sir, how do we get our money back?"

"Maybe you won't," I say, "because I do not mean to pursue it. But I suggest the boy who took it mail it to the boys he took it from."

"We'll recognize his handwriting."

"He can get his mother to type the envelopes."

"Then his Mom will know."

"She'll kill him."

"He'll never do it."

"Maybe," I say, "he will. Because if he does he will choose himself better. He'll feel good. He can write if off as an adventure he should never have taken."

"It's lunchtime, sir."

"Remember," I add, "I don't mistrust all of you. And remember you're only a thief if you continue to steal."

On the way down to the dining room, a husky kid sidles up next to me.

"Sir, you know who did it, right?"

"Wrong."

"You have a pretty good idea?"
"No."
"I do. He looks terrible."

Tuesday of the following week one of the boys comes up to my desk as soon as he enters class.
"Sir, I got my money back."
"In the mail?"
"Yes, sir."
"Me, too," another kid says.
The three of us look at the third kid who had money taken. "What about you?"
"I didn't get any mail."
"Maybe you lost that money."
"I could have. I lose everything."

 ## Choice

Choose to be aware of your consciousness. What an idea. Choice! What an idea. Like the thief, we can choose to change ourselves. We can choose who we want to be.

The child chooses.
The child changes.

There is hope, there is where it lies. I feel it when I'm with them; I see choice working through the year. It's the bonus we teachers get for spending our days among the children.

The child is what he's been made by his genes and environment: he is this accidental self, until the day comes when he transcends genes and environment and chooses himself. Until then, the child cannot be blamed for what he is. He's had no control over his accidental self.

Not everyone transcends. Some people never give a thought to actively participating in shaping the person they will be. They settle for what they have been handed. Religion, taste, prejudices, preferences, outlooks. They settle for it without ever realizing they've settled.

Others come upon themselves. Suddenly, they look upon themselves clearly, objectively. They look down and say, "Oh, that's who I am. That's what I'm like." In that moment, the chance to choose presents itself. With choosing comes change. Change is the escape route for kids with troubles.

The choosing of ourselves, I do believe, is our central duty. What we choose to be identifies our worth. What we're given at birth—skin color, money, poverty, connections—does not signify in comparison.

The task of the adult is to awaken the child, not blame him.

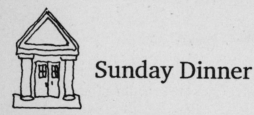 ## Sunday Dinner

1937. I'm eight years old.

Mama, the Duchess of Ursulines, gives me a dollar bill and one quarter. A lot of money. "Here, honey," she says, "go get yourself a nice meal."

This happens on Sundays. It means Dad is working at the Roosevelt Hotel and won't be home to eat, and Josephine doesn't see any sense in cooking for just herself and us kids. She means for me to head straight for the Port Elizabeth, that's a restaurant two and a half blocks from our house on the corner of Esplanade Street where the streetcar stops.

At seven years old I know a lot about good food. Mama's girlfriends are all French ladies married to the headwaiters and chefs of the best New Orleans restaurants. Everyone agrees, though, that Mrs. Ciel, the Austrian, the owner of the Port Elizabeth, is the best cook of all.

The front door brings me right into the bar. Some people sit there on stools and eat their meal without interfering with their drinking. They eat and drink and stare out of the window at the tall, fat palm trees growing on the neutral ground across the way. Don't picture those slender South Sea island palm trees. These are stout, thick; they grow straight and are always filled with dates and bristling with dusty, spike-tipped leaves. These look more like Japanese warlords walking two by two down the neutral ground.

Just past the bar are four tables, two to each side. I walked through them into the narrow corridor that makes you feel as if you're on an old steamer churning down to Argentina. To the left and the right are enclosed rooms, tiny cabins just big enough to hold a table and four chairs. On the wall of each is a button to ring for the waiter, and above the button a silver-colored machine about as big as a jelly mold with a sign that says *Violin*. Under *Violin* is a push slot that is supposed to take a nickel. But it never works.

"Hello, Ronald."
It's Mrs. Ciel. She's a pretty woman, buxom, rosy cheeks and she has blue-green eyes. She doesn't look slick like Merle Oberon, but I do understand her to be good-looking.
"Mama didn't cook today, Mrs. Ciel."
"You mean you want a meal for yourself?"
"Yes, ma'am."
"Come on, honey. I'll put you in the back booth right next to the kitchen."
The back booth is one of those small, all-enclosed rooms. She puts me back there because she doesn't want me to spend my money tipping any waiter. This way she'll wait on me herself, step right out of the kitchen with the food.

"How much you got, Ronald?"

I open my hand.

"Lord, you gonna be rich," she says looking at the dollar bill wrapped around the quarter. "You sure squeeze money tight."

She counts it.

"You want chicken or veal, honey?"

"Chicken."

"Okay. Here's your napkin."

All the great cooks in New Orleans refer to their cooking as chicken or stew, or bisque or soup and let it go at that. Of course, they prepare their chicken a dozen different ways but it's always, "You want the chicken?"

For ten minutes I eat French bread and butter and pretend I've sailed halfway through the Gulf of Mexico on my way to buy bananas. Then Mrs. Ciel emerges from her low-ceilinged, smoky, sputtering kitchen with a small dish of lettuce and tomato covered with oil and vinegar and dried mustard and chives and a big dish of melting-off-the-bone smothered chicken in a pool of amber gravy that makes French bread dipped into it taste like a banquet.

"How you get the rice so yellow?" I ask.

"It happens like that, Ronald. You gonna like it. And eat your snap beans. I cooked them with a little salt pork."

"Yes, ma'am."

"I'll go get you a Coke."

I concentrate on the food.

Lebat is standing there in the doorway in the middle of his talking before I know he's there. Lebat is a small, long-faced black man who cleans up the dishes and takes care of the garbage for Mrs. Ciel.

By the time I get adjusted to him, I hear him say, "—and sat just where you're sitting."

"What you talking about, Lebat?"

"The murder," he says.

He talks softly and quick but he pauses a lot in between what he says. I can listen to him and not lose track of my food.

He says, "He came here to eat before he killed all those people, Ronald. You know him."

"Maybe I do," I answer. My third-grade teacher at St. Augustine's is Sister Angelica. About three weeks ago her brother came to visit our classroom. He looked like a murderer.

"I know it," Lebat says. "They made me a detective."

I say, "What?"

"The police. Kept asking me questions but I wouldn't answer. One of them hit me on my shoulder. But I wouldn't talk."

"About the murder?"

"Yes."

I remember Lebat doesn't talk much to grown-ups. They make fun of him because he's simple.

"Why wouldn't you talk?" I ask.

"He'd come kill me."

His brown face is shiny with perspiration and his lower lip hangs down and his eyes move about.

I ask, "You knew him?" as I try the snap beans.

"Yes," says Lebat. "And he knows me."

I ask, "How much you get for being a detective?"

"Nothing. But I got a badge."

I don't say anything but he knows I don't believe him.

"Lebat!"

It's Mrs. Ciel.

"You leave Ronald alone!"

He peers down the corridor to the bar in the front and disappears.

That quick, Mrs. Ciel is in the doorway. "He's bad, Ronald. You hear me?"

"Yes, ma'am."

"Don't you ever follow him."

"No, ma'am."

"You need more bread?"

"No, ma'am."

She steps into the kitchen and right back. "Here." She puts some more bread and butter on the plate.

"Thanks."

In a minute, Lebat is back. He's put on a black rubber rain slicker. The kind that make you sweat. "I got my badge."

"Let's see it."

He has it. It's dented but it's real.

"I gotta go deliver some food. But when I come back, I'm gonna get you some peaches off the tree."

I know the tree he's talking about and I know the peaches.

"They're always sour."

"They're suppose to be, Ronald."

"Peaches are suppose to be sweet and juicy."

His eyes stop moving about.

"You're suppose to eat bitter, Ronald. God wants you to take the bitter. Look for it. Look for it and eat the bitterness. It's good for your insides. I'll get you some."

"Lebat!"

He doesn't look for Mrs. Ciel.

He leaves.

I finish my Coke and jiggle the ice.

"How you doing?"

"I ate everything, Mrs. Ciel."

"You liked the chicken?"

"Yes, ma'am. Real good."

"Okay. Next time tell your Mama to give you a dollar and a half and you'll get dessert."

"Don't need any, ma'am. The Coke was fine."

I get up and leave.

Plain Talk

I'm in the alumni office of Courtney Iglehart, wise and gracious Courtney. I've dropped in for a respite.

"Hello," she says.

"Hello." I sit down.

"Baz," she says, "what would you do—" She stops to get it straight in her head. We have the habit, now, with each other, of jumping right into the middle of a conversation. "I know this young woman, most becoming in all areas but one. She acts too aggressively, too assured. She's too opinionated for others. Would you tell her?"

I say, "If you told her and she listened, you could change the rest of her life. You could make the rest of her life better."

"I think that would happen. I'm sure it would. Should I tell her?"

"If this young woman were your daughter or niece or sister, you know you could hurt her. It could hurt her to know you see her so clearly."

"I know. Criticism is not what she wants. But it's what she needs."

She answers a phone call, and when she is finished she turns with a smile to me and says, "Well?" She's so well-mannered. So simple and refined. After a conversation with her I feel I've spent a week at Hyde Park.

"I think the first thing to consider is this: Let's say you tell her of this flaw; let's say she listens, she understands, and she *agrees* with you."

"That would be wonderful."

"The question is—could she do anything about it?"

She thinks a bit.

She says, "Because if she can't, why hazard hurting her?"

"Yes." I watch her think and then I say, "You know, you've put your finger on the most sensitive area of teaching."

"You mean talking straight to kids?"

"Yes. Plain talk."

"Parents talk plainly to their kids."

"That's true. But if a mother tells her son, 'You're eating like an animal!' nothing much has been risked, first of all because his mother said it, and second, because it goes in one ear and out the other. What if someone outside the family were to talk plainly to a child? To begin with it would bear more weight. It would be the outside world, the real world speaking."

"You mean, should a teacher do it?"

"That's what I wonder about. Kids are so vulnerable. The more affection they have for you, the more they relate to you, the more chance there is of their listening to you."

"And the more chance of your hurting them."

"Exactly. If one feels the slightest risk of doing that one holds back—and yet..."

"I know," she says. "There's the chance of doing so much good. Of changing a life for the better."

"Especially with fourth-graders. Nine years old, ten years old, that may be the last time to reach a kid directly, to talk to him plainly without creating lingering adult embarrassment. Fourth-graders may still be open to suggestion. And most important, they may still be young enough to do something about it. They're what Carlyle calls 'fictile'—clay in the process of being molded."

"Courage is always best."

"You think, Courtney?"

"I do."

I realize I'm late for class. "Oh, my Lord," I say and run out.

The Homonym Game

By God, one-third of the spelling mistakes fourth-graders make are homonyms. I discovered that this morning and this afternoon we devised a new game: HOMONYMS!

It's great.

The class divided into two teams: The Maps and the Windows. Each week we'll use the last fifteen minutes of our second history period to play it.

To begin I choose four or five sets of homonyms from a dandy grammar book I found, printed in 1865. There are some amazing words in that book. Let's say the first set is *time* and *thyme*. I don't define the words, I only say the sound: *tim*. Since this homonym is moderately hard for fourth-graders, instead of giving them the minimum number of points if they get it right, three, I tell them it's worth six points.

Let's say Maps has first cracks.

They have first chance to try for the points. If they want to try, one member or more of their team raises his hand. They cannot confer.

"I'll try, sir."

Good. To win the points this boy must define and spell each word correctly. If in the process he uses the word *like*, he gets fined one point. "Thyme is...ah...like...ah..." One point is fined.

As he is defining and spelling the words, the rest of the children write them down in a special place in the back of their class book. They write down both homonyms and next to each they write a clue to help them remember which is which:

time—get up

Something like that.

If Maps declines to try (if you try and fail six points are deducted from your team's score), the Windows can give it a try.

What if both teams decline? I give them a clue. "You all know the t-i-m-e word. The second one has something to do with cooking. Now it's worth only five points. Maps? No? Okay, Windows? No? Okay, here's another clue. It has an h and y in it!"

"I got it!"

"Maps?"

"Yes. t-h-y-m-e!"

"That's it! Give Maps five points!"

 # Discipline

Young scholars need affection as much as they need clear explanations. They need calm to settle their young fidgets. They need humor to keep up their spirits. And they need discipline.

A set of written-down rules has its bad points.

It allows teachers who don't mix discernment with their discipline to treat all kids the same. "What's good for one is good for another" is not true with children. Thoughtfulness can make a child disorganized. Highmindedness can make a child dress shabbily. Those children should not suffer from teachers following the letter of the law.

Children need discipline but grown-ups are often more severe on children than they are on each other. When I break a dish nobody remarks on it. I don't, my wife doesn't and neither do my sons. But when my sons were children, if one of them dropped a dish, I'd say, "What are you doing?" and my wife would say, "You have to be more careful," and my other son would say to his brother, "You dope!"

A teacher with too much Roman *gravitas* in his personality can be rough on a child filled with the mercury of Greece. The teacher wants an outline, the kid pours forth imagination. As much as it's necessary for a child to understand an outline, that's how much it's necessary for a teacher to understand not everyone is alike.

"The first job is to discipline!"
That's wrong.
A teacher's first job is to create a place for the child, a place the child wants to come to every day. Get the kid to want to come and spend the day with you and discipline follows.
Children do have faults that must be corrected. The best way to walk the path to perfection is in deep, humane conversation with fault.

Discipline is an art.
Experience helps, so does low blood pressure. With experience one learns to be simple. A fine actor is a simple actor. A good backhand in tennis becomes simple once you are doing it properly.
Don't allow them the opportunity to get into trouble. That's so hard to remember.
Take the kids out to the field the moment they arrive in the gym. Have the equipment ready. If you're not ready, the boys start to fool around and then they are punished for fooling around.
Start class crisply.
Why can't I always remember that?

Several teachers I've known attended strict schools as children. Schools of shouting, smacking teachers. One or two remember it fondly. Their outlook is severe. They think the kids give them too much guff.

I can't remember a kid giving me guff.
I've upset some children, I remember that. Frustrated, perplexed kids reduced to bad manners, I remember that.
It's not guff, though.
It's hurt and fear and pride.

 ## Sensitivity

I'm in the classroom alone looking out of the window at the grimy snow on the deck below.
Ernest comes in.
The intractable Ernest.
"Sir?"
I turn round most formally.
"What do you want, Ernest?"
He doesn't answer. He has a way all his own of reacting to a direct question. He blinks his eyes in such a way it makes you feel he's shrugged his shoulders and said, "I should think you know the answer to that."
"You should be in art."
"I know, but—well—Frank told me you're going to give me an extra assignment."
"You'll have to write a letter of apology."
"To whom?"
"Frank, Ernest!"
"For what?"
"Ernest, get out of here."
"Okay. Okay. I punched him during recess but he was calling me names."
"You knocked him to the ground for calling you a name?"

"A Martian. He called me a Martian."

"And for that you struck him to the ground?"

"That's how it worked out."

"Why didn't you call him a name back?"

"Didn't think of it."

"Don't you think you overreacted?"

"My mother says I'm sensitive."

"Sensitive!" I'm almost out of my shoes.

"Take it easy, sir."

"Does a sensitive person crush his classmate to the ground, Ernest?"

"He hurt my feelings."

"Ernest, there are two kinds of sensitivity."

"I didn't know that."

"One kind is being sensitive about yourself. Things easily hurt you, you get easily upset, your feelings are tender. That's what most people think of as being sensitive."

"I agree with that."

"Well, it's not worth much."

"It isn't?"

"No. And it's not rare. Most everybody, everybody here on Earth and everybody up on Mars, they all have it. What's rare is the other kind of sensitivity."

"What's that?"

"Being sensitive about others. Always keeping in mind what will hurt others and trying to avoid it."

"I get it."

"Considering others."

"I get it."

"Their feelings, not yours."

"Okay, okay."

"That's rare."

"Like Jimmy."

"Who?"

"Jimmy. He lets everybody call him names."

"No, Ernest, that's different."

"He could be, sir. He could think, gee, that guy needs to

call me names so I guess he has to do it."

"Ernest, go to art."

"If I go now, Mr. Bechlof will get mad."

"That's okay with me."

He begins to leave and then turns round and hesitates.

"Sir?"

"What, Ernest?"

"I mean, do I have to?"

"Yes."

"I mean write the letter. Can't I just shake with Frank and make it up?"

"Maybe."

"Because I listened to all that stuff you said."

"That was big of you."

"So?"

"Okay. No letter. But next time you hit someone I'm calling your mother and talking to her about sensitivity."

"That's fair."

"Goodbye."

"Thanks."

My Faults

I was too tough my first and second year.

I often think of those poor children. From the beginning I was good at the clarity part, I explained well and the kids listened. It was the disciplining. I yelled too much. Too often I got mad.

It isn't necessary.

Much happier, that's how I feel now that anger is behind me.

Pressing too strongly when I think a child is on the verge of a breakthrough—I've mentioned that flaw. And ego trips, I've covered that in passing. It wasn't often. I do remember, though, that awful personal insult I felt when a boy I had taught so well had the audacity not to learn. That was terrible.

Try as I might, there is one bad habit I've yet to break.
First, I fool around in class.
I'm as bad as the kids at that.
But that's not the bad habit. I think it's good to fool around; it breaks up weariness and boredom and introduces laughter and glee. It clears up a groggy head.
What I do wrong is to insist, once the joke is made and they are laughing, they stop grooving and resume work immediately.
I do.
The boys can't believe it.
My feeling is we've had our laugh and now let's get back to work! Now!
They don't see it that way. They want to ease back into industry. And there I am saying, "Now!" No, I don't get angry. But I am a pain. I perplex them. They want to please me but it's hard to stop having fun.

Patience may be my other flaw. Too much patience.
A few parents and one or two teachers fault me on it. They feel I don't expect as much as I should from some children. They feel the child who isn't working hard senses my easy way and takes advantage of it. They could be right. I see it as a close call. I decided long ago I'd rather gamble on having confidence in the kid than on treating a kid too harshly.

Not always gentle.
The heart of many teaching situations is reached with firmness. There are times when one must be mentally tough. When the class is just about to understand why three-fourths is seventy-five percent, why one, in the sense

of a whole, is one hundred percent—at that time, the atmosphere must thicken, they must stay focused, and the teacher must move from gentle to firm.

Opera Notes

My class mother comes to visit.

"Mr. Bazarini, you haven't taken the kids anywhere this year."

"To tell the truth, Gladys, I've been ailing."

"Nonsense. You look ten years younger than your age!"

While I try to figure out how she knows my age, she sits and says, "This is New York City! We must take advantage of it!" Someone is always saying this to someone else in Manhattan. It's a habit we provincials have, a conceit to look upon our grumbling city as a beauty who must be enjoyed.

She goes on. "You took my older son's class to an evening of ballet."

I get it. Tone is the game.

"It's my thin southern blood, Gladys. A midwinter trip through the city makes me blanch." As I'm saying it I see I'm making no impression. "But you're right," I go on, "let's do something."

"What about an opera? One of our mothers is connected," she explains.

"Which?"

"Tales of Hoffman."

"Grownup."

To mind comes the sumptuous production given it by the City Center. I remember the second act completely revolving around the boudoir, the black silk stockings, and the *décolletage* of Giulietta, the courtesan. As played by Joanna Simon, that is a lot of revolving.

She reads my mind.

"Nine-year-olds are courageous," I say.

"It's settled!"

"If," I respond, "three or four of you mothers take us there in your cars."

"We'll take them and bring them home."

"Fair enough."

The trip over is sleek—a step into waiting station wagons and a step out before the doorway of the theater. It is there that trouble waits. Twenty adventurous kids, an assortment of parents, and one teacher, together we discover that neither the ticket office nor the Opera Guild has ever heard of us or of St. Bernard's School.

Perplexed, I can think of nothing better to do than herd the children out of the cold and into the lobby of the theater. I am absolutely no good in these situations.

Several of our mothers explain our predicament to several members of the theater staff and have no success. We're told we're not expected and there simply are no tickets for us. But then, a calm-voiced, pleasant-faced attendant appears, takes on our problem, solves it and leads us with dispatch to the third tier.

I can't resist asking her, "Why could none of the others help?"

She answers, "I've only been working here three days."

It's possible she didn't understand my question.

In addition to being efficient, she is considerate and takes us up in the elevator instead of by endless steps. Consideration in the Big Apple is rare. As we approach our seats I can think of nothing else. She, on the other hand, continues busy. By the time I have come round, she has seated eighteen of my charges in the front, overhanging row of the stratospheric third tier!

I can't believe what I see. Leaning forward out of their chairs, their china-boned heads and childish shoulders suspended sixty or so feet in space, they look, all eighteen, so perishable. It must have been then I dropped the British cavalry officer's gloves my wife had bought me for a special treat from Bloomingdale's. Fortunately, an elderly woman retrieves them and hands them over with a cryptic, "I bet they're yours."

The gloves, the suspended children, the curiously alert elderly woman—all of it must have made me gasp standing there, because a mother grabs my elbow and leads me to a second-row seat saying, "The boys won't fall, and besides, back here we can bop them on the head with our umbrellas."

The first act comes and goes. I remember nothing more than the greenness of the tenor's voice (that could be the reflection of my bile) and the lugubrious basso flinging parts of a body to the floor. It makes me wonder whether my boys, once toppled, will bounce, break, or squish.

During intermission, they scatter in a rush for whatever delights the concession counters and labyrinthine corridors offer. I try not to look like a teacher. There is a benign pose I assume at such times. It's copied from an old-moneyed friend. Mostly it's a look of vague interest in everything, as if one were delighted at existence for all its efforts to amuse but actually too world-weary to enthuse. Who knows if those around me actually get all of that—I have my doubts—probably a becoming malaise is about it.

Of course, we all settle nicely into the second act. A boudoir is a boudoir even to a Middle-Schooler.

The third act tries patience. True, the woman who plays the consumptive Antonia is a fair-sized bit of humanity; it isn't difficult to accept her lingering on and on. But even justified lingering is wearing. Five of my boys bolt. I find them playing shootout across the elevated open spaces of the exposed upper lobby.

For me, the jig is up. I have to become teacher and take my chances. It isn't too bad. To the distant strains of tubercular lament the boys and I face off.

The sight of me means nothing to them. They sense my hands are tied. Teachers don't scream in the lobbies of opera houses.

I motion in a pontifical way for them to approach. The novelty pleases Sam. He is the first to join me on the bench.

He says, "You couldn't take it either, right?"

I answer, "I was doing my best."

Frank joins us. "I had no idea it would be like this."

"Like what?"

"So boring, sir. This isn't for kids!"

I begin to think perhaps I'll take tomorrow off.

But I wake surprisingly refreshed and find that my step, as I enter school, has a spring. During ten extra minutes we have before art, I try to drum up conversation with the boys concerning the opera but they're more interested in playing Gladiators.

After school, Gladys arrives eager to discuss the event. "We made a mistake, didn't we?"

"What makes you think that?"

"I've never known a class to get up out of their seats in the middle of an aria to play 'Got-cha!' in the lobby."

"That is unusual."

She says, "We should never have taken them."

"I disagree, Gladys."

"But they were bored."

The afternoon sun finally makes it into the room. I pull down the shade and say, "It wasn't Disneyland but we knew that before we decided to go. We decided deliberately to stretch their heads. That's what school's all about. Challenge. Each day. A concept in math, a relationship in

English. That's the game."

"But, Baz, they thought it stank!"

"Some did."

"Most."

"And they were right. I mean they had a right to be bored. We can't argue that. But there are other thoughts to consider. A few liked the opera. We introduced them. We should be proud."

"Three out of twenty?"

"Not bad. Three this year, three more next."

"And those who don't enjoy opera," she says, "will they ever learn to sit patiently?"

"Let's hope."

She relaxes and adds, "We can't always be attending something we like."

"Good point," I say. "I'll explain that to them."

She asks, "Do they listen to a teacher when he discusses such things?"

"Moralizes? Yes, with great interest if they sense they can debate the issue. I mean to bring up the members of yesterday's audience who were irritated by the boys' behavior—the special trips they made to be there, the scarce money some paid."

"Oh, my."

"Kids spoil some things. It can't be helped. And kids delight, too. Some of the grown-ups were pleased to see them."

"I enjoyed it all."

"I noticed," I say, "and I was envious."

"Of what?"

"Exuberance. Mine's trickled away."

Rejection

Marvin has lingered in the classroom.

"Go on, Marvin," I say. "Go to Science."

He's acting tough. He says, "I don't mind going to Science."

"Good. Then go. You'll be late."

He's a husky kid. Also, very smart.

He gets up from his desk and I lose track of him. Immediately I'm absorbed in organizing a fourth-grade Favorite Books list requested by Al Meyer, our librarian.

Ten minutes pass.

I look over my shoulder and there is Marvin, strong, super-bright Marvin, in tears. He is seated on top of his desk, his chest heaving, his hands covering his eyes.

I say, "Marvin, you love Science."

He heaves once and says, "I know."

I cough nervously and say, "You love Mr. Millhouse."

"I know," he says, making fists to push into his eyes and squeeze away the tears.

"Oh," I say.

I stop to think why he could be crying.

He answers on his own. "It's after Science, it's recess. I don't want to go to recess anymore."

"That's why you're crying?"

"Well, I know you like us all to go because there's no one to mind us if we stay here." He says this with great understanding, pushes his dark hair off his forehead, and begins to cry some more.

"Marvin, we can work something out."

"You *think!*" He means I'm a fool to be so simplistic.

"You can spend recess time in Al's room."

"Who?"

"Mr. Kilborne. You like being with the older boys and Mr. Kilborne won't mind."

"What I'd like is to go to recess!"

"Then what are we talking about, Marvin?"

"We're talking about how mean Jerry is."

I begin to understand. Until two days ago, Jerry used to sit next to Marvin.

"You're mad at Jerry because he wanted to be moved to another desk?"

"Away from me. And now he won't play with me at recess."

"Marvin, he likes to get into the football game."

"Sure!" Marvin's eyes have had a good bath, they gleam through his tears. "Because he thinks the games I make up are weird. He thinks I'm weird."

I get some tissues to blot his fair face.

"Marvin, Jerry *wants* you to play on his team during recess. He thinks you're the best football player in the class. But, instead, you want to play these unusual games you make up."

"You like them."

"But I'm a little weird."

He laughs but not for long. He says, "You're always telling us it's not wrong to be different, stuff like that."

"It isn't. That's your privilege, Marvin. But you can't expect to be loved for it."

He looks at me hard as he tries to figure that one out. I say, "You purposely think of wild things to do and then expect, no, demand Jerry like you for it. And you also make fun of him."

"Jerry?"

He can't believe I said that. He can't believe he can like Jerry as much as he does and anyone could think he makes fun of him.

"You do. If he doesn't answer just perfectly in class, you always make some comment, Marvin."

"I'm just kidding. He knows that."

"No, he doesn't, Marvin. And you're not kidding."

His anger makes his tears stop. "You think I'm making fun of him?"

"Because you like him."

He almost understands what I mean. The feeling that happens within him when he teases Jerry almost makes him understand.

"I do like him," he says.

"And you want him to like you."

"Yes."

"And he doesn't as much as you wish he did."

"He won't come to my house anymore."

Marvin's not angry anymore and he's not crying.

"Marvin, I think I know what you're doing."

As I say the words he determinedly looks not at me but straight ahead. Some bright kids do that when they're listening their hardest. They don't want the social contact anymore. They want to concentrate on the thought that's coming. "Because you like Jerry more than he likes you, you're trying to show him *why* he should like you."

I pause and he doesn't like it.

He wants me to finish the thought but I want him to relate more to me.

He does.

He turns reluctantly and asks, "Why is that?"

"Because you're smart."

"I'm trying to tell him he should like me because I'm smart?"

"Yes."

125

"But that's not nice." He means he'd never do that because it wouldn't be nice.

"You're not being mean. You're offering your best present. When you correct Jerry in class, you're saying to him, 'Look! I have a little something you don't have. Together we'd be unbeatable!' "

"We would be!"

"No doubt in my mind about it. But you'll have to stop teasing him."

"He teases me."

"I know. And you have to put up with that."

"Why should I?"

"Because, right now, you like him more than he likes you."

"Yeah. That's true. That's gotta change."

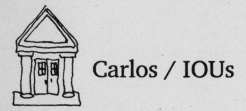

Carlos / IOUs

To keep the boys in line, my greatest help has been Carlos, the killer. Before the first week of school is over, I introduce the boys to him. "He's deadly, fellows. You can't escape from the reach of Carlos. He'll gun you down no matter where you hide."

"Who is he?"

"You never heard of Carlos!" I say. "He's famous the world over and he works for me in this class."

"What does he look like?"

"Nobody knows what he looks like. But you'll know it when he gets you."

Now some of the boys are beginning to smile and snicker. "Get us for what?"

"For being bad, that's what. Here is how it will work. Each time you're bad I'll yell out 'Carlos!' Then, next to your name right here on this list by my desk I'll put down a circle. That's a Carlos."

"So?"

"So? If you have a circle next to your name you can't begin your homework with the others. You must do an extra problem first." (Every day in the fourth grade they have a 'prep' period at the end of the day. They begin doing their homework assignments at that time and finish up at home.)

"A hard problem?"

"Extremely hard," I say. "Sometimes you can waste ten minutes of your homework period doing it."

"How can you get a Carlos?"

"It's easy," I say. "If you don't do an assignment, you get a Carlos. If you talk, yell, leave your seat, make a mess, push somebody, eat like an animal, dirty your paper."

"I got it."

"Here's the good part." They are all ears. "You can get out of a Carlos if you have an IOU. Isn't that great?"

"What's that?"

"If you have an IOU from me it means 'I owe you' one escape from Carlos. For an IOU you get one Carlos cancelled."

"How do you get IOUs?"

I answer, "By drawing a great picture for your history notebook, by helping someone, by cleaning the lunch table."

"Doing great stuff."

"That's it."

"What do they look like?"

"I give you a special slip of colored paper with my sign on it. You keep it and when it is time for you to do a Carlos you bring it up and I take away the Carlos."

"Neat."

"How many can you get?"

"As many as you can."

"How many Carloses can you get?"

"Well," I explain, "you work them off at the end of each day so they don't accumulate."

"What if you got ten in one day?"

"Nobody's that bad," I say. "But if they pile up faster than you can get rid of them, the limit is five. When you get five you have to sit out recess."

"You mean that, sir?"

"Carlos is tough."

They think it all over.

"Sir, if let's say I get three or four IOUs. Can I sell one?"

"No, no selling. But you can give one, or lend one to a friend in trouble."

"What if he doesn't pay back?"

"That's your risk."

They mull over risks and friendship.

"Sir, what's the most IOUs anyone has ever gotten?"

"Forty-one."

"But, sir, if you have a lot what's the use of keep trying to get more?"

"You mean with lots of IOUs in your pocket you could afford to be bad."

"That's right. Isn't it?"

"No. Because of the prize."

"Prize?"

"Yes. And the record book. The one with the most IOUs gets his name in the record book and, besides, on the last day of school we draw for the prize."

"What is it?"

"Something wonderful. On the last day, for every extra IOU you have, you get to put one slip with your name into the hat. One IOU, your name goes in once. Twelve IOUs your name goes in twelve times."

"What was the prize last year?"

"A National League baseball."

"Make it American League, sir. I hate the Mets."

Nerves

I'm on the phone with Raymond's mother. I've called her twice before to ask her to come in for a conference. Both times she wasn't feeling well.

"Can we talk about it over the phone, Mr. Bazarini?"

"Sure."

"What is it?"

"Raymond doesn't seem quite happy, ma'am."

"He's a serious boy, Mr. Bazarini. I'm afraid the entire family is. Is his work satisfactory?"

"Yes. He's super-bright. Words—words are so natural to him. He must read a lot."

"Everything. I sometimes worry about it. He always has his stack of books. Is it anything serious?"

"He's been crying."

"Oh?"

"For no good reason that I can see."

"You mean he just bursts into tears?"

"No. Usually a boy teases him. But the kind of teasing that most boys don't even notice works up Raymond instantly. I feel as if he were a bird, a young bird who can't fly, who is always on the verge of falling out of the tree."

"You must try to catch him."

She knows what I'm talking about.

"I do. I have caught him several times."

"Because if you don't he'll throw a tantrum. Worse, really. He falls apart," she says.

"I've heard about that."

"From the third-grade teachers?"

"From all of his teachers."

"They've warned you."

"They've sought to help me help the child."

"I'm sorry. I know they must."

"Your son seems unusually nervous, ma'am."

"I know. He has the thinnest of coverings. I hope you find a way to help him."

"I'll catch him."

"I'm grateful for that."

Silence.

"Ma'am, is there something else that could be done?"

"You mean psychiatry?"

"No. He—he's just so nervous."

"I don't think a psychiatrist would help."

"Neither do I."

"Our doctor and two other doctors suggest Ritalin. Have you ever taught a child taking Ritalin?"

"Yes. I had a kid years ago who couldn't sit still."

"They put him on it?"

"Halfway through the year."

"It helped?"

"He could sit still, but he wasn't the same. He seemed somehow sad. Wistful, I guess."

"I'm suspicious of it, Mr. Bazarini. We, the family, have decided to live with Raymond the way he is and hope he gains some calm without the use of drugs. But maybe that's asking too much of the school?"

"No. Not so far. *If* I catch him in time."

"His outbreaks in the other grades were disruptive to the class, I know."

"No, he hasn't done that yet."

"That's good news. What do you do?"

"It's funny. So far I seem to sense when frustration is building up in him. Something tells me to check him out and there he is turning red in the face, on the verge of an explosion."

"What do you do?"

"I just say, 'Raymond, it's okay.' He sputters out, 'But, sir, how can I—' 'It's okay, Raymond. Whatever happened is over. Just stay calm. It's okay. Raymond, it's okay.' That's about it."

"And it's working?"

"It doesn't make him less nervous but it stops him from breaking up."

"Will that suffice?"

"God..."

"Oh, I know," she says, "you'd like him merry and smiling. But he isn't that way."

"He's a fine boy. He knows about everything."

"He does." She falls silent.

I don't know what else to say. "I thought I'd check in with you."

"Thank you, Mr. Bazarini."

Traditions

The detail of a work. How the elements of a painting, a musical, a play, a cathedral are woven into the structure is so enriching.

Texture.

The texture of a school.

Every Friday the school assembles together in our small gym, the gym with the stage. A simple prayer is said with bowed heads. No kneeling. Whoever doesn't wish to say the prayer refrains, and no one notices. Then a school song is sung. We have a modest booklet that gathers all of our school songs, songs written by class masters of times gone by. Quaint pieces but all our own.

That done, everyone sits on the floor and waits for The Alligator to be presented. This reptile, a small stuffed one with a red ribbon around his neck, is presented by a few selected members of the class that won him the week before. It is given to the class found to be the neatest during the week just passed. A minute skit or a poem is rehearsed and offered. The name of the winning class is saved till last. Once the announcement is made, a representative of the winning class, one or two, ascend the stage, shake hands with the members of the presenting class. Two first-graders going down a line of four sixth-graders shaking hands is an endearing sight.

The captains of the teams deliver game reports.

The president of the debating society delivers his report.

The headmaster gets all he has to get off his chest.

Finally, the main attraction begins.

Each class shares the task of entertaining the school on one Friday of the year. Plays are most popular. Sometimes concerts are offered. Sometimes poems. Satires, too. Once, a pantomime.

Tradition. School songs. Entertainments. The Alligator.

In December of every year the eighth grade, the graduating class, presents a full-length Shakespearean play. It is cast the previous spring, mulled over during the summer, rehearsed in the fall, staged, costumed, and presented as the highlight of our holiday season. Stretched beyond their means, the eighth-graders dig deep within themselves for understanding and emotion and enunciation worthy of the Bard. Frightened and overwhelmed, they grow the courage needed to propel them onto the stage. It's at night, everyone is dressed up, their older brothers are in town from their boarding schools. A stalwart tradition!

The Literary Magazine. It comes out twice a year. A slim, elegantly, simply printed and bound booklet containing writing efforts of a couple of boys from each class section. Essays, poems, stories, memories. How important it is. How meaningful to a youngster to see his writing in print. What confidence it produces.

No school should be without a literary magazine. And not a purple-mimeographed stapled stack of sheets. No. Every school should find the money to do a handsome printing. It doesn't take much. It's a lift to young writers.

Medals.
Prizes.
Speeches.
Concerts.

Every school should have its traditions. If they don't, they should begin them tomorrow. A school should be a family and it should have texture.

When a child does something specially grand during the week, call him up on stage and give him an orange. Get one of your mothers or fathers to be there on Friday to present it.

One Friday, we had Theodore White come on stage to give out oranges and apples to the kids. The week before, Mr. White had won the Pulitzer Prize for his book *The Making of the President, 1960*.

Mr. Westgate explained this to the boys and then said, "So we have a special prize for Mr. White."

Having said that, Mr. Westgate walked into the wings and came back with Mr. White's prize—a watermelon.

You don't have anyone who has won a Pulitzer Prize? Start a literary magazine, and a few years down the road, you will.

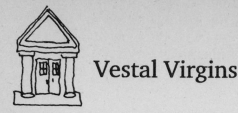

Vestal Virgins

The school year is coming to a close.

We are in the middle of Roman history.

The topic is religion, and that leads us to the Vestal Virgins.

"Yes, I'm sure they wore long dresses," I say, "and their job was to tend to the sacred fire of Rome. They were priestesses."

"What's a virgin, sir?" Ernest asks.

"Usually the boy who knows the answer to that question is the one who asks it, Ernest."

Ernest gives his snorting laugh, and two or three young savants join him. I ask him to tell us.

"A virgin," he explains, "is a lady who has never been with a man."

Now, about seven are laughing and snorting. Another seven are looking wide-eyed, perplexed and extremely young. I imagine them saying to themselves, "Never been with a man? They must be little girls born in ladies' prisons. Ladies' prisons must be filled with virgins."

I explain.

"Ernest means a lady who has never had sex with a man is a virgin. She's still pure. She's still innocent."

Taylor says, "In other words, sir, they never get married."

"That's about it."

Clifford says, "Men, like, are rotten, right?"

"Sort of," I say. "Now these Vestal Virgins signed up for thirty years. Usually they signed up at a young age. Well, chosen. They were selected from good families. Young girls."

Ernest zeroes in. "Were they virgins before they signed up?"

"That's the point, Ernest," I say. "Once you stop being a

virgin, that's it. You had to be a virgin in order to become a Vestal Virgin."

"So what's the point?"

"A priestess should be pure!"

"Okay. Okay."

"The interesting thing is, after thirty years they could retire. And then they could marry if they wished."

Clifford says, "So they all got married, right?"

"No. That's what's so curious. They almost never married."

Ernest says, "It was like a habit. I get it."

"Could be," I say. "Consider, if they entered the order when they were seven, they'd be thirty-seven when they retired. And—"

"And they get a pension, right?" from Clifford.

"Maybe," I say. "But I was going to say that at thirty-seven a woman is still young, still young enough to marry and everything. But few of them did."

Clifford says, "I think Ernest is right. They got in the habit of being pure. They get married, they got to have kids and all that stuff, they figure they're better off."

By now the entire class is getting the idea and they are very interested in the subject matter except for Sal, in the corner. He's bored stiff. He's thinking of his baseball cards.

"Sal," I say, "what would you do?"

He thinks a bit. Then, "Don't you have to be a girl to be a virgin?"

"Yes. But if you were, would you get married?"

"You mean after?"

"Yes, after you retire?"

"No. I'd just go fishing. My grandfather retired last year and he gets to fish every day in Florida. I'd go fishing."

"Alright. The topic for next week's composition will be Vestal Virgins."

Clifford says, "Sir, give us a break!"

Ernest says, "I'm not going to pretend I'm a girl."

"You don't have to. Pretend you're her father. Pretend you're the young man who loves her and doesn't want to see her go."

Sal asks, "Could I pretend I just retired?"

"Yes, Sal. Pretend you're a retired Vestal Virgin on a fishing trip."

The Vestal Virgin
Craig T. Peters

Sarah was tired of doing her mother's housework. The only way to avoid it was to be chosen a Vestal Virgin and keep Rome's sacred fire burning.

Sarah was starting to cook supper, when a lady dressed in white came in. Sarah had never seen her before. "Would you like to be a Vestal Virgin?" asked the lady.

"Oh, yes, please! I'd love to!" Sarah replied. She went with the lady to the convent where she lived twenty-nine years.

There were many virgins there, but Sarah's best friend was Ruth. One day, Sarah couldn't find her. She had to, for it was Ruth's turn to tend the fire. When Sarah at last discovered her, Ruth was in the arms of a strange man!

All day Sarah hoped that the Mother Virgin (the Virgin in charge) would not hear of this incident. If she did, Ruth would be beaten and buried alive. For weeks, Sarah did not see Ruth. Until she glimpsed her outside the convent one day. Sarah supposed Ruth had been beaten and buried. "Ruth!" she called. "What happened?"

Ruth told Sarah her thirty years were up. She didn't have to be a virgin any longer. She had been married in the chapel of the convent.

Sarah was glad Ruth was alive. Still she wished Ruth hadn't left. Then Sarah was told her time was up. "So that's what it's like being a Vestal Virgin!" she thought, as she walked away.

Gifted Child

The kids we reward, the ones we praise—they are attentive, perceptive, and retentive. They listen, they learn, and they remember. Good manners and neat dress and good speech make it all the better. They get the high marks, go to the first-choice schools, and are welcomed by the Ivy League colleges. They are the best bets.

It makes sense.
The criteria are sound.
What doesn't make sense is *when* we expect a child to show these qualities. I mean, there is nothing wrong in a child displaying these attributes early. What's wrong is our demanding all children display them early or suffer the consequences.

The early birds are to be congratulated; they are indeed good bets, excepting those few who have been coerced into high industry and will burn out.

There are actors who audition for parts with great facility and never go beyond that depth during rehearsals. The finest actors and actresses often audition poorly: they are awkward, they are nervous, they are so aware of the depth of feeling and thought actually needed to bring the character to life—well, it makes them unable to do anything smoothly.

Kids are like that. The finest minds cannot always perform well early on. There is too much bubbling inside. Too much imagination and introspection are getting in the way of slick industry. It may create within them a need for more play, for more daydreaming, for more resting. Modes of thinking could be forming in a child's young mind as he unproductively sits there that will allow him one day to reorganize an industry, or compose a concerto, or judge in a court.

Parents and teachers want children attentive and retentive by the fourth or fifth grades. Boarding schools want proof, documented in the dossier, by the eighth grade. If it isn't there by then, the child is unacceptable. Colleges demand high SATs. Whoever doesn't get them is made to feel stupid.

What else do boarding schools and colleges have to go on? These scores, an essay, a letter of recommendation, perhaps an interview, and no more. They can't possibly wait any longer to assess the child.

That's true.

I understand.

This is also true. Gifted children can easily be late bloomers, and a few of the early achievers can easily be run-of-the-mill, children good at producing what's expected when it's expected.

Some of our best prospects are hindered by a system that favors routine efficiency, a system that denigrates those who can't demonstrate measurable distinction early on.

The world is impatient.

Thoughtful minds, cautious, analytical, philosophical minds, are penalized by this impatience for growing root rather than leaf.

 Belmont Raceway

It is springtime. The Belmont Raceway Morning Workouts is a great trip to take the boys on. The track doesn't open until mid-May, which almost insures beautiful weather. I enjoy everything about it. Usually five mothers come with me. They arrive in front of school at seven-thirty with their cars. I divvy up the class and we motor off to Long Island to find the racetrack.

The mothers are always puzzled.

Why go to the racetrack?

How does it tie in? Math? Science?

I answer, "I like to watch the horses."

My students live in the middle of Manhattan, most of them within walking distance of the finest science and art museums in the world. I assume the parents take them to these places of culture and learning. I don't feel the need to do it myself. Besides, I'm not comfortable in a museum with twenty children. I'm not comfortable crossing the street with them. As for being in the museum with them, I don't know how to control them outside of class. I don't. Within class I get control without thinking about it. In the street or in a public place, I'm absolutely no good at it. Also, there's so much traffic in New York. I worry about them. They spill about like puppies tumbling from a box before you know it. There's the weather, too. For most of the school year the weather in Manhattan is dreadful. Once I make it to school, get out of my dripping raincoat, soggy shoes, and damp scarves, I don't much like the idea of going back into the gloom.

When May comes, I feel differently. As King Lear says, I'm reborn. I can't wait to drive the highways to the raceway. I can't wait to get there, and once we are there the puzzled mothers don't want to leave. Once they move into the open, terrace cafe for breakfast and see the immaculate track spread before them, they understand why I come. It is a place of beauty. Suddenly the world is as it should be. The sky is blue and shining bright, the track is a comforting oval, an ample, unencumbered, continuous path. It is the serene place to appreciate the beauty of the running horse.

Mind you, we've come for the morning workouts. Not the

races. The yelling crowds aren't here in the morning. We are just children, and mothers, and grooms and jockeys and trainers. We haven't come to watch a thoroughbred pressed to the limits of his speed. During these workouts they will walk about and sometimes prance. They will saunter off away from us to the starting gates and in a minute or two they will come running by, running not full out, not strained, but rather in a frolic—handily, breezily, with a joyful spirit as if they were playing a grand game.

The boys love it.

The mothers are mesmerized.

Nobody wants to leave.

We have breakfast right there at track's railing; we taste orange juice, hear snorts and whinnies, and watch trim and muscled four-legged wonders bound by.

I say, "Let's go."

Boys and mothers say, "No!"

"It's time to visit the stables."

"Oh!"

Nearby they notice the motorized trolley of connected wagons. We climb aboard and slowly and noiselessly we are pulled round the stables to see these gorgeous creatures being washed down, combed, petted. We see them in their stalls patiently, majestically looking out, thinking, I'm sure, of tomorrow morning when they will circle and kick and snort once again.

When we return from the tour of the stables, there is always the hopeful question, "How long are we going to stay, sir?"

"This is it. Back to school."

"Aw."

And always a mother says, "I didn't know about this. I've got to come back. I didn't know this place existed."

Christmas Eve / Christmas Day

I'm nine years old. Back home in New Orleans. Christmas Eve.

The sky is gray.

I'm sitting next to my older brother, Junior, on the front steps. His face could look like the sunshine when he wants it to, but now he's deadly serious.

He says, "Cold enough to snow."

I can't believe he said it. "In New Orleans? That would be a miracle!"

"What's wrong with a miracle?"

That's just like Junior. He brought a sick bird home and took care of it on our back porch. He did that once. It died. Junior didn't cry. Mama and my fat Nanane and I cried. We couldn't understand why Junior didn't cry. But, then, none of us ever brought a sick bird home.

"Jesus can make a miracle," I say.

"I'm ready," he says.

"Don't they have to be far away?" I ask.

"Miracles?"

"Yes."

"New Orleans is far away from China."

"Does it snow in China?"

He says, "I don't know."

We are seated on cold cement steps surrounded by houses with peeling paint. Junior is thinking it through.

The next day.

Christmas morning.

I wake up to the miracle words, "It's snowing!" And then, "Ronald, it's snowing!"

How strange.

And stranger still, I don't spring out of bed. I linger on the radiant face of my mother looking out at the snow.

All my life I'd heard, "You'll never see snow on Ursulines." But, oh, it's snowing.

Mama doesn't know what to have me wear. Nanane doesn't know how to caution. "Don't catch cold, Ronald!" doesn't seem powerful enough. Two pairs of socks for certain. Two sweaters. Two scarves and a pull-down woollen hat. "Over the ears!" cries Nanane. "Over the ears!" sounds right.

But first, breakfast.

"Snow kills southern children!"

Nanane tans creamy bowls of boiled milk with a spurt of Union coffee and then Junior floats a pat of butter on top of his and mine. We dunk in slices of French bread. Out the window the delicate snowflakes are falling. What will it feel like against my cheek?

Junior leads the way.

He's carrying a bucket Mama rinsed and dried.

We step out the front door.

The snow has stopped.

It had stopped. I would never feel it against my cheek. I had pictured how I would walk through it, how I would offer my face. Together, Junior and I look into a southern Christmas Day without snow.

We walk down the block to look round the corner. It's all we can think to do.

"Did you see it?" a neighbor asks.

"Yes," says Junior. "I saw it."

The neighbor is satisfied. We cross the street and walk the following block to Governor Nicholls. It isn't there. The sun is beginning to shine. The air is empty. Turning back to walk home, Junior says:

"Look, Ronald. On the steps."

On all of the steps before the houses there is a haze of white. One by one we scrape them clean. It makes a gritty half-inch at the bottom of our bucket. No kin to the wonder we had hoped to walk into.

Things go funny.

It was there and then it isn't.

All was possible and nothing is possible. Christmas Day is cold enough but it's a proper southern Christmas without snow.

I get a pasteboard fort and a box of soldiers. Mama and Dad give me that. Nanane gives me three dollars. Junior gives me skates. Then we have a nice meal and he leaves to play with his older friends.

Later, I'm sitting alone in the front room waiting for Junior to return. Outside I hear a neighbor call to someone else, "It's a miracle! A miracle!"

In my mind it means, "It's snowing!" In my mind it means Junior had gone and found the snow. In the Vieux Carré it's not unusual to hear people talk of miracles. Gri-gri, secluded patios, evil eyes, spells—to talk of miracles is not unusual.

Then I hear, "The Blessed Virgin! On Governor Nicholls!"

Mama is at my side.

"Let's go, Ronald."

We put on a coat and a hat and leave. On the front step we see Junior. "Let's go," he says. "Around the corner."

On the corner of Governor Nicholls and Marais, gathered in the dark night, a hundred people stand watching the roof above the Acme Dry Cleaners. It is an old, one-storied creole building with the cleaners occupying the corner half and a family living in the other half. It's humble in the gloomy night, fragile, exposed to the chill of December. What little there is of a moon is behind its high peaked roof. Now and then it gleams through passing clouds.

We join the others.
All is quiet.
The lady next to us whispers, "That little girl was walking by and saw her on the roof holding Jesus."
I look at Junior and then look at the roof and see the Blessed Virgin holding the baby Jesus in her arms. Mama squeezes my hand. Then two men with flashlights arrive and shine them on the roof. Mary and Jesus disappear. There's nothing but a life-sized chimney in their place.
A few people laugh but most are disappointed and walk away. Mama and I go with them. She thinks it best not to talk about what happened. She takes from it what she needs and goes to sit in her room to have a Coke and smoke a cigarette. I tell Nanane all about it while she sits with me in the kitchen saying her beads.

I go back to the front room and wait for Junior. When he comes in, he sits and puts his arm around my shoulder.
Things are good.
I say, "What do we do now, Junior?"
He says, "We wait for the snow, Ronald."

Revelations and Recognitions

About fifteen years ago I was given two gifts, two insights that occurred a few weeks apart. My way of teaching was changed forever.

The hero of the first experience is a fellow named David King-Wood, head of the English Department. It happened the day after the performance of our annual Shakespeare play. He has been directing them for twenty years. I had been backstage with him at the Barbizon Plaza's theater, helping out.

Have I mentioned David before?

As a young man he was a member of the Royal Shakespeare Company in London. Starred opposite Vivien Leigh.

We had been like two old troupers the evening before, enjoying the backstage exhilaration, as excited as the young men in multicolored garb, who, painted and whiskered, glued and rouged, walked about astounded by their transformation.

David had come into teaching mid-life. Once in the colonies he decided, I presume, to choose the simpler (and perhaps more dignified) life of teaching children to use and cherish their English language properly.

I am his fan for many reasons.

He is a cultured, handsome, poised, and endlessly cheerful man of high temperament. I like that. The temperament, too, God, I like that. He is refined and yet a pugilist in an instant if his principles are attacked. He is good-natured but capable of delighting one with the delight that only caustic comment can accomplish. Above all, he is gracious and he brings good manners and polish and dignity to his role of teacher.

Half of whatever is good about my teaching I owe to David King-Wood. Not that I've ever seen him teach. In all of the years we've plied our trade together at St. Bernard's I have never been into one of his classes. But we've talked about children and their needs and their eternal promise of better things to come. There is a gentility about David, it surrounds him when he is with the children. He keeps them in order and yet he brings all of himself to class. He comes to school to live each day with them.

In my subconscious, without being aware somehow, I had felt this quality about him for years. Then, the day following the Shakespeare play, I was in the hallway of the Upper School and I saw him there talking to his charges, and I saw that *friendship*. Nothing unusual was happening, teacher and students were chatting about their concerns, but I was aware. I felt the friendship that united them: they were like partners in search of content and style. The school day became more than drills and skills and industry. It became a time to expand.

Three weeks later, I received another gift.

It was that time of the week when my fourth-graders left me to go to Art. They lined up and exited and I followed along. From the hallway I could keep an eye on them until they entered the art room.

Every week, twice a week, we did this.

They left and I watched.

Once they were safely with Mr. Lukach, I'd turn and go back to my classroom. As I did this, the second-graders would usually enter the hall on their way to early lunch. Second-graders are appealing little devils. Without thought, I formed the habit of waiting for them to pass by.

146

I wouldn't enter my room immediately. I'd remain in the hall to see their mugs, pat their heads, greet and joke and tease.

One day, after my class entered Art and before the second-graders came by, I must have fallen into a reverie. I was lost in what thought I have no idea.

The next thing I knew I was staring into the face of a second-grader. I was saying to myself, "This child has his own joys, his own fears, his dreams and anxieties." I no longer thought of him simply as a child to teach. He became different. He was a boy with an entire existence surrounding him, a multitude of experiences, memories, pressures, puzzlements; all of the parts that make him who he is. "I must remember that," I told myself. "I'll never know all there is to know about him, but I must remember that this depth of life comes to school with him."

This took a moment.

These thoughts shot through my head and I became suffused with the complexity of his young life. I knew this child. Somewhere in my mind I must always remember that each day he confronts more than my expectations.

It happened in a second and the next second I realized I was looking into the smiling face of my son, Nicolas, then a second-grader at St. Bernard's.

He was the child I had been looking at all along. From within my reverie I had not known that. From within my reverie I saw the depth and the intricacy of the child. Then I recognized my son.

There is Peer. Dark-haired, brown-eyed.
He sits dejectedly at his desk.
"What's wrong?"
He relates his day of setbacks. He's done poorly on a history test, he's argued with a friend, he's lost his baseball glove.

I ask, "What can you do to fix it up?"
"I don't know, Dad."
"Will you try?"
"Yes. But there's a lot across my mind."

"A boy's will is the wind's will,
And the thoughts of youth are long, long
thoughts."

—Henry Wadsworth Longfellow
"My Lost Youth"